THE AOVIA PRINCIPLE

THE AOVIA PRINCIPLE

A Path of Unlimited Potential

Margrit Goodhand, LCSW, CAP

Where Authors are Family™
Columbus, Ohio

The views and opinions expressed in this book are solely those of the author and do not reflect the views or opinions of Gatekeeper Press. Gatekeeper Press is not to be held responsible for and expressly disclaims responsibility of the content herein.

THE AOVIA PRINCIPLE: A Path of Unlimited Potential

Published by Gatekeeper Press
2167 Stringtown Rd, Suite 109
Columbus, OH 43123-2989
www.GatekeeperPress.com
Copyright © 2020 by Margrit Goodhand, LCSW, CAP

All rights reserved. Neither this book, nor any parts within it may be sold or reproduced in any form or by any electronic or mechanical means, including information storage and retrieval systems without permission in writing from the author. The only exception is by a reviewer, who may quote short excerpts in a review.

Front cover Photography by Markus Aman

Library of Congress Control Number: 2020945673
ISBN (paperback): 9781662904523
eISBN: 9781662904530

DEDICATION

To my family and friends,
My faith family,
All sent-away kids,
And my muse, Mani.
You came to me in a whisper
And asked,
"Did you forget? Did you forget?"

CONTENTS

PREFACE XIII

ACKNOWLEDGEMENTS XVII

INTRODUCTION XIX

SHADOW TAG XXIII

CHAPTER ONE - THE PROBLEM:
THE PAIN OF FEELING STUCK 1

CHAPTER TWO - THE SOLUTION:
A PATH OF UNLIMITED POTENTIAL 21

CHAPTER THREE - STEP #1:
ASK WHAT TYPE OF SUCCESS YOU WANT 35

CHAPTER FOUR - STEP #2:
OBSERVE WHO YOU ARE 55

CHAPTER FIVE - STEP #3:
VISUALIZE YOUR DESIRED GOAL 81

CHAPTER SIX - STEP #4: IMPLEMENT
SPECIFIC STEPS TOWARD YOUR GOAL 107

CHAPTER SEVEN - ANALYZE PROGRESS MADE 121

CHAPTER EIGHT - SCRIPTS FOR
SELF-HELP & TIPS FOR HAPPINESS 127

EPILOGUE 135

ABOUT THE AUTHOR 137

ENDNOTES 139

BIBLIOGRAPHY 143

PREFACE

If you feel stuck, suffer from burnout, or lack a clear purpose for your life, I wrote *The AOVIA Principle: A Path of Unlimited Potential* for you. This book can serve as a guide to help you bounce back from a crisis. You can use it by itself or as a supplement to traditional therapy. I began writing it during a time when I met all of the above criteria. Despite having a successful career, I felt burned out, stuck at a dead-end, and had a severe case of compassion fatigue.

Being on call 24/7 for ten years had caught up with me. I was exhausted physically, mentally, and emotionally from the disruptions of my circadian rhythm. Then a surgery triggered the re-experience of a repressed traumatic childhood event. I decided to go on a sabbatical and resigned from my position as clinical program director. In my thirties, I had ditched earlier attempts of writing professionally in order to become an expert in another field. During my time off, I realized that I had become just that: a seasoned clinical social worker with a postgraduate degree and a professional license to practice therapy and provide clinical supervision to postgraduates.

Through a series of synchronistic events during my sabbatical, I discovered that the desire to be a therapist and writer had been inside me since I was seven. I had imagined myself in those roles while sitting at an old, black typewriter without paper and missing the A-key. In retrospect I understood that I had been trying to heal from my traumatic experiences as a *Verschickungskind* (sent-away child) at the age of six while placed in a large group home in Sankt Peter Ording. That place had been marketed as a recovery retreat on the shore of the North Sea in Germany.

Instead of recovery at that facility, I experienced terror and a sense of complete severance from my family and community, accompanied by an unbearable emotional pain that manifested as a painful constriction in my throat. As a six-year-old, I did not know what I have come to understand today: I had been subjected to what psychoanalyst Alice Miller described as poisonous pedagogy, a practice that used authoritarian methods designed to break a child's will.[1] For example, I was placed in a double-bind of having to choose between two forbidden acts—going to the bathroom *and* wetting my bed. The only possible outcome was punishment for breaking the rules.

Years later, a major part of my healing was discovering the *Verschickungskinder Deutschland* (Sent-away children Germany) on social media. When I learned that there had been 8-12 million of us between 1945 and 1990, I began to view my early childhood from a brand-new perspective.[2] I connected to others who had been affected, began to support related research, and got involved in activities to prevent such atrocities from ever happening again. Finally, it included writing this book and starting to work again—this time as an independent social work contractor. In that role,

I was able to create my own schedule and limit my number of referrals.

My writing this book is a direct result of becoming receptive to previously unknown information. Despite well-meaning but ill-suited advice, I neither created a self-help book offering promises of instant results nor wrote from a scientific angle to be passionately challenged and debated. Instead, I did what I encourage anyone in distress to do at the beginning of a major endeavor—get in touch with their inner self in order to effectively improve their life and the lives of those around them.

We must take care of ourselves to avoid burnout. I had lost the connection to myself during an upwardly mobile career that no longer worked for me. *The AOVIA Principle: A Path of Unlimited Potential* presents a reliable method to reinvent yourself from the inside out by connecting to your highest purpose.

ACKNOWLEDGEMENTS

I cannot express enough gratitude to the members of the Dunedin Writers Group for providing me with valuable feedback during my readings. Specifically, I want to acknowledge the following writers who reviewed specific segments of my work and offered valuable insights: Jon Mike Miller, D.N. Bedeker, Thomas McGann, Alexis Langsner, Kip Koelsch, and Joanne Griggs. I especially want to thank Jennifer Sloane and Toby Morgan for their professional copyediting, line editing, and proofreading of my work. Additionally, I want to thank Sarah Duckworth at Gatekeeper Press for her outstanding work as my author coordinator. Further, I want to thank my amazing son Markus for taking the inspiring photo of Marco Island and letting me use it royalty free for the book cover.

Moreover, I want to express my gratitude to the following professionals who reviewed and validated my work in the areas of their professional expertise: Dr. Michael P. Strolla, Dip. ABAM, FASAM, Medical Director of Healthcare Connection and ACTS, for my describing the benefits of neurofeedback and what it can offer people, and Dr. Steve Jones, Ed.D., America's leading hypnotherapist, for my explanation of hypnotherapy and its benefits. Lastly, without intending to sound pretentious, I want to acknowledge my indebtedness to the originators of the US Declaration of Independence for so elegantly capturing the truth of our unalienable rights in that document.

May we all have the courage to claim these rights of Life, Liberty and the Pursuit of Happiness because they belong to everyone. As a US citizen, I still believe in the promise of a New World with unlimited potential for those who not only dream but dare to realize their dreams with the help of a mighty power greater than themselves.

INTRODUCTION

Scientists have not yet been able to identify what consciousness is; however, there appear to be two main camps. In classical physics, consciousness is generally viewed as a deterministic part of the physicality and functioning of the brain. Social scientists, such as Alexander Wendt, promote a view of consciousness through the lens of quantum consciousness theory and regard it as a primal macroscopic experience. Such a view allows for making sense of phenomenon such as intentional behaviors, free will, teleological reasoning, and even our ability to change the past.[3] This book is not entering the scientific debate or escaping to a blind belief system. Instead, it presents a systematic method to liberate yourself from the pain of feeling stuck, suffering from burnout, or lacking a clear purpose.

During the first chapter of my work, I explore "The Problem: The Pain of Feeling Stuck" and begin to consider the following question: If children unconsciously play themselves into the future by visualizing, can adults do the same to reach desired goals? During the second chapter, I present "The Solution: A Path of Unlimited Potential" and introduce the *AOVIA Principle*, that, like every principle, is a fundamental truth. The acronym stands for the steps *Ask, Observe, Visualize, Implement,* and *Analyze.* Although we might have different reasons for feeling stuck, the path of unlimited potential can work for everyone.

Being on that path means becoming receptive to a nonlocal but all-pervasive intelligence that works on your behalf by arranging synchronistic events instead of forcing your own solutions with limited information. As you read this book and implement the steps during each chapter by processing the information, answering relevant questions, and completing the exercises, you are bound to discover a higher purpose and vision that will guide you on your path of unlimited potential. Each of the chapters ends with a "Dare to Imagine" exercise and a page for entering Reader's Notes. Both are designed to stimulate your imagination and creativity.

In order to experience the limitless, we must transcend normal day-to-day functioning. What is considered "normal," is not necessarily sane. It never was—and will never be—sane to enslave others, commit genocide, rape, sever limbs, mutilate genitals, or break the will of children in the service of fascism or any other political system.

What makes these acts of insanity is that they create unspeakable suffering and loss of life. Such acts violate all principles of natural law and unalienable rights so beautifully crafted for the US Declaration of Independence. Unless each of us works to disrupt the cycle of violence perpetuating egregious abuses, we are responsible for its continuation.

In light of my experiences as a six-year-old Verschickungskind subjected to a poisonous pedagogy under the guise of education and medical care, I pondered whether my will had ever been broken. After reviewing my life, I concluded "No, despite the barrages of abuse and neglect aiming in that very direction and the impact causing me injury, they left enough battle scars that remind me each time I forget." What about you?

SHADOW TAG

Margrit Goodhand

"My shadow is bigger."
"That's because you're fat!"
"I can make it smaller."
"Let's step on our own shadows!"
"It doesn't work."
"I can use my left foot to step on the right one!"
"I can, too."
"Let's play shadow tag!"
"How?"
"Whoever steps on the other's shadow first, scores!"
And so, it goes....

CHAPTER ONE
∞
THE PROBLEM: THE PAIN OF FEELING STUCK

Nothing Will Work Unless You Do
~Maya Angelou

Imagine taking steps to avoid your shadow. Perhaps you, like I, tried it as a child when playing with friends. If so, you quickly learned that it does not work because your shadow is an inseparable part of you and follows wherever you go. You also learned that you could step on part of your own shadow. Finally, you discovered that playing shadow tag allows you to step on another's shadow and make them "it."

Just like our physical shadow, we have a psychological shadow that is part of our mindset. That mental shadow contains the unacceptable and forbidden characteristics we have learned to hide from our ordinary consciousness in order to function in a given environment. As a result, it leads us to project these characteristics onto others. The only way to change that shadow is by changing our character or location in the light of understanding. To get rid of it, we have to be in a totally dark environment. Of course, that is not possible, excluding a coma or death.

Our mental shadow—like our physical one—follows us wherever we go. It is held in place by our defense mechanisms that prevent us from facing our current reality in order to make effective changes. For example, we might justify smoking pot by saying, "Everybody does it" or rationalize, "We all had to lie or go to jail." Both these statements are evidence of distorted thinking. Not *everybody* smokes pot, and not *all* had to lie. A more likely explanation is "I smoke pot because I like it" or "I chose to lie to avoid negative consequences."

Because our use of defense mechanisms is subjective, they can be positive by ensuring we maintain a desired status quo. In contrast, distorted thinking is always negative because it fosters false and delusional beliefs that prevent positive changes. My life situation led to writing this book because I felt hopelessly trapped. I no longer gave a damn; I wanted my life back. Qualified to assess, diagnose, and provide mental health treatment, I knew I was in trouble. I had burned my candle at both ends for too long and lost my zest for life. I was in a position where I could relate to Maya Angelou's *Nothing will work unless you do*.[4]

In addition to carrying out my regular administrative, supervisory, and clinical tasks, I had been on call 24/7 for almost ten years. I was exhausted from the endless demands of producing more with fewer resources. While the money was good, anticipated pay raises or bonuses had lost their appeal for me. I had had enough, decided to go on a sabbatical to regain my balance, and then resigned from my position as Clinical Program Director.

In a way, I was challenging fate to reroute my life. I had always wanted to be a professional writer. I also decided that I wanted to get elective surgery on my upper lip to remove a small cyst due to a scar from a fall as a child. Things got worse before they got better. The operation triggered a re-experience of my initial trauma. The difficulty of formulating words during the healing process was debilitating and triggered past memories that I had never dealt with. The difference was that now I was an adult with mature coping strategies, including journaling.

While continuing to journal, I also tried my hand at writing short stories, essays, and parables. The support from members of the Dunedin Writers Group provided valuable feedback to improve my writing technique. Because the group promoted the publishing of its members' works in anthologies, seeing one of my stories in print encouraged me to continue. In line with my interest, I decided to write a self-development book and explore the following question: If children unconsciously play themselves into the future by visualizing, can adults do the same to reach desired goals?

As a result, I developed the AOVIA Principle *(Ask, Observe, Visualize, Implement, Analyze)* as a guide for use during a step-by-step process described in chapters three through six. By choosing my subtitle, *A Path of Unlimited Potential*, I deliberately challenged my existing cognitive ability. Whereas the information I had stuffed inside my brain was correct, it had its limits, and combined with having lost zest for life, I felt stuck.

I knew that in order to proceed, there was only one place I could go: To the layers below my conscious mind, an area that had been identified by Freud to hold 90% of largely untapped capacity not fully utilized. Since then, neuroscientists have increased that estimate to 95%, leaving the conscious mind with a measly 5% of thinking capacity and the 95% governing ordinary consciousness.[5] To my knowledge, no therapist providing psychodynamic (insight) therapy focuses on the unconscious as an anatomical structure, unless a person has a neurological disability. We presume that the subconscious holds information that is not our current awareness, and that the unconscious holds socially unacceptable ideas, our drives, and traumatic memories. According to Jung, the personal unconscious is part of a larger collective unconsciousness containing information from our ancestral evolutionary history.[6]

During my sabbatical, I was ready to explore what was influencing me and how I could recreate myself to live up to my potential. In preparation for this book, I tried to write from different perspectives. After well-meaning feedback from others and much deliberation, I decided to stand in my own power. I used what I found helpful and discarded all other advice. While appreciating assistance with technique, I was the expert when it came to subject matter. I had lived my own personal and professional development and knew what had worked and what had not. I had ditched earlier writing during my thirties in order to become a specialist in another arena, and now I had become one—in the field of clinical social work. Consequently, my book neither offers promises of instant results nor is it written from a scientific angle to be fiercely challenged and debated.

Instead, it encourages anyone in distress to do what I did at the beginning of a major endeavor—get in touch with their inner self in order to effectively improve their life and the lives of those around them. You cannot be effective unless you start with yourself. That connection to myself is what I had lost during an otherwise upwardly mobile career. We see others not the way they are but the way we are, as a reflection. Like our shadow, we can only change the world by starting with ourselves. Ultimately, we tend to link with kindred spirits as shown in my following parable:

The Gates of Plentiville
Margrit Goodhand

The world is our looking glass. While much seems to happen around and to us that we have no control over, the world reflects who we are on the inside to the outside. Therefore, a good character is conducive to experiencing genuine and lasting fortune.

Plentiville had the reputation of being a wondrous village of magical plenty because of its smart and hardworking inhabitants who had kept it that way for a thousand years. And that is exactly why Amos and Reuben wanted to move there. They had grown up together and were ready to leave their old village of Testville in search for new opportunities.

Amos looked for a fresh start because he had recently lost his family in a house fire. It was too painful for him to be reminded of his misfortune every day by remaining in the old environment. Like Amos, Reuben wanted a new start but for a different reason. He had developed a habit of getting into trouble with the other villagers in Testville because of issues he considered to be petty. For example, they yelled at him when picking an apple or two from their trees or for just having fun. The latter was scaring little children, especially girls, by making awful faces and chasing them until they ran back home screaming.

As Amos and Reuben walked together on the dusty road to Plentiville, they shared their hopes and dreams for a new beginning until reaching their destination. Inside the first gate sat Eli, a wise man with a turban, white beard, and weathered face, whose job was to be present all day in order to welcome the travelers. Upon arriving at the gate, Reuben hurried to pass through first, with Amos following him at a respectful distance. Eli rose from his seat and, with a big smile, stretched out both of his hands to greet them. Reuben hastily grabbed his right hand for a traditional handshake, but Amos thoughtfully waited for Amos to extend his hand to him first.

"I welcome you to Plentiville. My name is Eli, the gate-keeper. May I ask what brings you to our village on this beautiful day?" he inquired.

"I am Reuben, and this is Amos," Reuben answered while pointing to Amos. "We left Testville because we are looking for a better life. Tell us, what kind of people live in Plentiville?" he inquired, having taken the liberty to speak for Amos.

Now, as already mentioned, Eli was a wise man. Therefore, he wanted to probe a little deeper into the character of the two men who wanted to enter his village. He chose to start with Amos by asking him to step aside far enough so Reuben would not hear their conversation and asked,

"Amos, what type of people live in the town where you came from?"

"Oh, they are friendly and generous, but I ran into the misfortune by losing my family in a house fire. Because the painful memories of seeing my poor family dying in the flames do not allow me to stay, I am looking for a place to start over," Amos disclosed, hoping that Eli would understand his situation.

"Well, that's how the people are here, friendly and generous. Welcome to Plentiville," Eli said with a big smile, exposing two rows of pearly white teeth while embracing

Amos. He kissed him on both cheeks and then pointed him to go into the direction of the second gate while commanding the guards to open it, which they immediately did. After stepping through the gate, Amos was greeted by some villagers offering him refreshments and shelter.

Then Eli waved at Reuben to come over and asked him the same question:

"Reuben, what type of people live in the town where you came from?"

"Oh, they are nasty and selfish. They don't share from their plenty and spoil their children," Reuben answered, expecting that Eli would understand him without a doubt, which actually he did.

"Well, that is exactly how the people are here, nasty and selfish," Eli replied politely but with a frown because two wrinkles had formed between his bushy eyebrows. Then he pointed Reuben in the direction back to the first gate while ordering the guards to escort him out, which they immediately did. That is how Reuben found himself back on the dusty road while Amos had entered Plentiville where he began to prosper until the end of time.

#

As for Reuben in the above parable, the areas beyond ordinary consciousness hold the shadow for each person. We use conscious or unconscious defense mechanisms, with our ego mediating between our instinctual desires and our moral conscience to ward off excessive anxiety. As a result, we then project our undesirable qualities *onto* others or might accept their projections *into* ourselves.[7] These projections into ourselves become part of our mental shadow. Eli, the wise gatekeeper, was not about to let Reuben into Plentiville to wreak havoc by projecting his problems onto others. But he welcomed Amos, an authentic character who was ready to join a people who had made the village "a wonderful place of magical plenty."

Having already done work in the areas of transference and countertransference as part of my clinical training, I became interested in further exploring my own ego defenses of repression and projection as every therapist should. Trained clinicians agree that the prerequisite to someone recognizing their ego defenses is a feeling of safety. A threatening and judgmental environment is counterproductive to promote such inner work. Having extracted myself from an environment that made "the hamster run faster," I thought I was ready. But when I opened my personal Pandora's box, I got more than I asked for.

First, I was faced with the various manifestations of my personal shadow that, for the most part, I had safely tucked away. Then, while experiencing a period of normal confusion due to newly emerging insights that forced corresponding emotional and behavioral adjustments, I realized that I actually had a good foundation to explore the realms beyond my ordinary consciousness. As part of my preparation for getting credentialed as a Qualified Clinical Supervisor for post-graduate interns in Florida, I had already done some shadow work as part of my competency training.

I decided that now was the time to continue with that work and befriend my shadow to empower myself instead of unconsciously projecting it onto others. During that process, I began to view my development from a different perspective and in a brand-new light. Armed with a fresh understanding, I began to recreate my past with pieces from recently recovered memories. This process enabled me to be receptive to the unfamiliar and relationships that I had not known anything about. For example, a seemingly random conversation triggered my memory of getting in touch with childhood trauma.

Specifically, I had forgotten that at the critical age of six, I had been shipped by rail to a six-week placement in what had been marketed as a recovery retreat for children. During a routine TB tine testing in first grade, I had had a positive reaction. A follow-up X-ray showed that I had a spot on one of my lungs. While tests of mucus showed no active TB, I was severely underweight. That qualified me to be sent away to Sankt Peter-Ording, a large group home at the shore of the North Sea in Germany.

In that place, instead of healing, I experienced terror and a sense of complete severance from my family and community, accompanied by unbearable emotional pain that manifested as painful constriction in my throat. As a six-year-old, I did not know what I have come to understand today—that I had been subjected to what psychoanalyst Alice Miller described as poisonous pedagogy, a practice that uses authoritarian methods designed to break a child's will.[8] For example, I was placed in a double bind of having to choose between two forbidden acts—going to the bathroom *and* wetting my bed. The only possible outcome was punishment for breaking the rules.

One of my recovered memories is squirming on a hard mattress in the dark with my bladder hurting like hell. I felt confused and entrapped by having been forced to choose between two forbidden acts. It took some time for me to remember that, at one point, my early potty training took over and I went to the bathroom anyway, despite the warnings of older children as to the possible consequences. I now remember the tiles on the walls in the bathroom and struggling to find my way back to my bed in the almost dark room.

A vivid memory is being coached to smile by staff who took the photo in Figure 1; I was hoping for further attention and affection that never came. The darkness inside my eyes and the shadows underneath reveal my true condition. In light of my experiences, it is not surprising that at age seven, I played the role of a therapist and wrote imaginary books on an old typewriter without paper and the A-key on the left side missing.

Figure 1

In what I can only describe as synchronism, reports of about 8-12 million children having been sent to such places began to emerge on social media and websites. I established contact with Anja Roehl, also a *Verschickungskind* (sent-away child) and special education professional, who had initiated a citizenship research project for tracking down survivors and bringing the issue to the media's attention. Her goal was to get the German government and its collaborating agencies to acknowledge the suffering endured by the children and to make funds available for research, the processing of the traumatic experiences, and the needed networking among the survivors.

The typical age range of the Verschickungskinder had been 5-14 years.[9] Commonly shared experiences include public shaming, compulsory eating of unsightly and ill-tasting foods, being forced to eat regurgitated food, emotional abuse, corporal punishment, theft of personal belongings, bullying, and sexual abuse by staff or older children.

Additionally, postcards to families were censored, and little ones like me, unable to write, were left to their own devices sitting there with a pen and card, confused, and making a mess of things despite attempts of other children to help.

Recently, one of my clients, whom I must keep anonymous, experienced a catharsis that revealed why she felt nauseated when thinking about eating eggs or drinking red wine. "I was eight years old, had heart problems, and was underweight. I was sent away twice. I remember having to sit in mud baths up to my neck and being forced to drink chianti with raw eggs," she disclosed. Imagine a young child being subjected to such treatment without her parents.

And imagine schools, religious dioceses, and youth welfare offices referring, medical doctors ordering, and insurance companies funding 8-12 million children for six weeks to go to such places—sometimes up to four times. While various branches of government have already acknowledged that the Verschickungen have caused much suffering, all activities are still carried out by volunteers. This despite emerging information that high-ranking Nazis, who had killed Lithuanian Jews and euthanized children, ran such group homes, or provided medical services to the children after World War II.[10]

A second live Congress for the Verschickungskinder on the East Frisian island of Borkum is planned for September 2021. The goal is to provide resources for survivors to deal with their painful memories, learn about the historical context, mark a place of remembrance, and create publicity.[11]

I have agreed to be the US coordinator for the sent-away children in the United States in order to promote the interests of survivors living here.

As a mature adult, I began to explore how my experience had impacted me from a developmental perspective. Having discovered a new paradigm for my life, I confronted the existential questions: Who am I? What do I want to do? Who wants or needs what I do? How will they benefit from it? Working myself through many layers of peeling the onion, I began to grasp how this childhood experience had undergirded my developmental path and came up with the following answers:

"I am a licensed clinical social worker. I help others to feel better. I do that by rekindling hope and eliciting motivation in others using therapy, advocacy, and writing. What people want is to feel better about themselves and their lives. They benefit from what I do by feeling better."

After untangling myself, I had found hope at the bottom of my Pandora's box. I was elated to discover that the seed of my purpose had been planted during a significant traumatic event that I had been unable to process without adult support. No wonder I had been looking for love in all the wrong places. I felt a surge of new energy and sensed a promising path ahead. As a child, I had been forced to experience such intense pain that I could only cope with it by forgetting. Now I was able to embrace that child, validate her suffering, and honor her early attempts to play herself into the role of a healer. Like the rings inside the trunk of a tree, I finally experienced a conscious integration.

My overall life situation became more hopeful. As a result of my sabbatical, I had more time to spend with family and friends, and my circadian rhythm began to stabilize. I examined my early family and social relationships in order to get more information and initiated desired changes instead of waiting for others to do so. While writing this book, I started working in my field again, this time as an independent social work contractor. This allowed me to create my own schedule and set clear limits for the number of my referrals.

The 2020 Covid-19 pandemic delayed my snowbird plans. I was unable to leave my residence in Florida during the summer as intended to spend time with my family in Pennsylvania. Instead, I used the opportunity for face-to-face encounters using SMS, Zoom, or Jitsy Meet. For work, I was able to use Doxy.me to provide telehealth therapy to my senior clients, the population with the greatest mortality risk after getting infected.

Identifying the problem is half of the solution but formulating the other half can be challenging. To that end, it is helpful to look at the root of a problem. I discovered that just as children unconsciously play themselves into the future by visualizing, adults can use the same method to reach desired goals. When you identify your own reason for the pain of feeling stuck, you can liberate yourself, begin to thrive, and enjoy life. I was able to do exactly that while writing this book.

After identifying "The Pain of Feeling Stuck" as the problem in this chapter and presenting my own example, I encourage you to identify your reason for such a pain. In the next chapter, I will present "A Path of Unlimited Potential" as the solution. It is the AOVIA Principle, that, like every principle, is a fundamental truth. The acronym stands for the steps *Ask, Observe, Visualize, Implement,* and *Analyze*. But first, I provide you with a "Dare to Imagine" exercise to process important points from this chapter and a "Reader's Notes" page to capture your Aha! moments.

Dare to Imagine:

- The pain of feeling stuck as your problem.
- A psychological shadow reflecting your current mindset.
- Your shadow containing unacceptable, painful, and forbidden characteristics.
- Your shadow only changing when you, your position in the light, or the light itself changes.
- Using visualization to reach desired goals.
- Your mind comprising 95% of untapped capacity beyond ordinary functioning.
- The area below your conscious mind holding your shadow.
- Your shadow projecting your own limitations onto others.
- Others' shadows projecting their limitations into you.
- Projections preventing you from making positive changes.
- Facing your shadow as a liberating and empowering experience.

Reader's Notes:

CHAPTER TWO
∞
THE SOLUTION: A PATH OF UNLIMITED POTENTIAL

To Thine Own Self Be True
~William Shakespeare

The above saying was Polonius's last piece of advice to his son Laertes in Shakespeare's *Hamlet*. How is it possible that 95% of the capacity of the human mind is locked away below our consciousness but controls the majority of our thoughts and behaviors? Having only working access to 5% of our mind's capacity at a given time blocks any chances to experience unlimited potential. Additionally, the subconscious and unconscious areas of our mind do not use verbal language to communicate, as anyone trained in imagery knows.

The good news is that you can thrive on a path of unlimited potential by learning the language of the areas beyond your conscious mind. Doing so will enable you to connect to what scientists describe as a nonlocal domain of a unified field that, at the same time, exists everywhere as unlimited potential and manifests intentions. It is from that domain that pure intelligence organizes what is called a bubbling *energy soup* by binding quantum particles into matter such as atoms, atoms into molecules, and molecules into other structures.[12]

Initially, Freud used the terms subconscious and unconscious interchangeably to describe the area beyond the human consciousness. Later, Jung differentiated between the personal and the collective unconscious. For Jungians, the collective unconscious stores ancestral memories and images called archetypes.[13] Such images are templates that influence and even control human behavior. They include the gods of ancient Greece, the shadow, the anima and animus, the gods and saints of various religious traditions, and even the mother and father figures. In that way, everything we perceive becomes part of us and we of it.

Therapists trained in imagery know beneath ordinary consciousness communication occurs that is encoded in signs, symbols, images, and feelings. Without an ability to decode that language, its messages exert governing influences on our reality in the physical domain. They include flows of epigenetic modifications from our ancestors, arising from the stress of their hardships and trauma, even if our psyche appears to operate in a purely materialistic world.

Learning to decode such imagery and related feelings enables us to recover repressed memories, identify personal archetypes, face hidden shadows, and remove blockages that prevent us from living up to our full potential.

Basic methods to learn that language include journaling your dreams and working with a therapist skilled in that area. In my case, I had completed a workshop with a group of other people, led by my own therapist. During that process, we got to know ourselves better in a supportive setting by interpreting dreams and deepening our insights. This helped us to recognize and break chains of limitations and allowed us to move forward.

Your psychological shadow is not only all the hidden things you and your social environment finds unacceptable, it is also the stuff—and here comes the kicker—you *unconsciously* project onto others. The more unaware you are of your hidden motivations, the larger will be your blind spots that others can see, even when you cannot. It is not for the faint of heart to face their shadow. However, those who do experience a sense of unparalleled liberation and empowerment. In a way, you get to recreate yourself from the inside out. By looking in the mirror, you can see and let go of self-defeating coping strategies and make room for developing more helpful ones.

For example, I strongly disliked individuals who created chaos by breaking laws. I put myself above such despicable conduct. During my shadow work on projection, the truth feeding my disdain struck me. I, myself, was a lawbreaker without remorse. It was hard for me to admit that what I had been doing had adverse effects on myself and others because I was actually proud of it! I had found a way to illegally stream TV from all over the world to my heart's content by using open source media centers. With my IPVANISH VPN network encryption, I was able to change my own IP address frequently, making me undetectable.

My denial system was massive. I rationalized that paying for internet access was a waste of money because I could do all I want with 100 gigabytes of hotspot on two phones. *They* did not have the channels I want to watch anyway, especially ones from other countries because I love foreign movies. I justified that I was a smart boomer who learns from millennials. At least, I did not break into computers and mess with the dark web like they did. What motivated me to come clean was writing this chapter and really grasping that to continue what I had been doing was not in my best interest. It would have kept me stuck where I did not want to be—hiding and putting myself in harm's way.

I found that sometimes telling on myself is the best way to confront issues and offers others the courage to do the same. Part of my courage came from remembering an excerpt from Eckhart Tolle's *A New Earth* that I had read several years ago. Eckhart had been fascinated by an obviously mentally disturbed woman having loud and angry conversations with herself. He found himself hoping that he would not end up like her. Later, when looking in an actual mirror, he was shocked with the realization that he was already like her. He also had conversations with himself; the only differences being that his thoughts, driven by anxiety, never came out of his mouth.[14]

As a result of facing and befriending my shadow, I have become more accepting of others, without necessarily equating this to approval. I enjoy my improved live-and-let-live attitude because I know that the way we judge others says more about our own character than someone else's. Ultimately, we all get to experience the consequences of our actions. Spiritual people call it karma and scientists evoke Newton's third law: For every action, there is an equal and opposite reaction. I learned that when feeling too strongly about someone else, it usually has to do more with myself instead of that person and presents an opportunity for personal growth.

As previously mentioned, the mind *beyond* ordinary consciousness has its own language coded in signs, symbols, emotions, and images of significance. An example is the circle, a universal symbol representing totality and wholeness. An incomplete circle forces the psyche to perceive it as a *Gestalt* (whole perceptual structure) instead of accepting the incomplete line. Sometimes, information from your subconscious emerges spontaneously as a result of needing it. For example, you might automatically administer CPR to an accident victim although you did not remember the steps the day before during a conversation with a person whom you took a course with.

Additionally, we tend to blindly repeat lifestyle patterns established by generations before us in response to their environmental stressors by the mechanism of epigenetics. An increasing body of scientific evidence indicates that factors such as ancestral nutrition, trauma, stress, mental health, and addiction can modify gene expression.[15] The significance is that not only we but also our offspring might experience undesirable outcomes because of predisposal to addiction, obesity, anxiety, depression, or even psychosis.

In light of what you have learned so far, do you have the courage to confront your pain of feeling stuck? Do you want to start your healing process, get on a path of unlimited potential, and experience the joy of success? I will proceed to clarifying some terms for you now in order to avoid misunderstandings so you can move forward. For the purpose of this text, unlimited means no restrictions in terms of numbers, quantity, or extent. Potential stands for the latent qualities or abilities that may be developed toward achieving success. And because success represents the subjective means toward attaining prosperity, you must define it yourself.

As a step-by-step guide on your path of unlimited potential, I have developed the AOVIA Principle. The acronym stands for the steps *Ask, Observe, Visualize, Implement*, and *Analyze* that I used to organize chapters three to seven of this book. Chapter eight is a bonus titled "Scripts for Self-Help and Tips for Happiness" where you can find additional resources. As you engage in processing the information and completing the assignments, you are bound to find yourself on a path of unlimited potential. The five action statements that guide the implementation of the AOVIA Principle are as follows:

THE AOVIA PRINCIPLE

Step #1: **A**sk what type of success you want.

Step #2: **O**bserve who you are.

Step #3: **V**isualize your desired goal.

Step #4: **I**mplement specific steps toward your goal.

Step #5: **A**nalyze progress made.

At this point, I will introduce you to three important concepts. Understanding them will help you to avoid self-sabotage during interactions with others. The first concept is that you are the seed of unlimited potential; the second concept is trusting others according to their nature; and the third concept is treating others with unconditional positive regard. These three concepts will not only give you the wings to deal with resistance but also improve your character in the process. We need resistance to raise ourselves above limitations. Neither birds nor planes can fly without it!

You Are the Seed

You cannot get on a path of unlimited potential by only reading about it. Instead, you must get on that path yourself. You are the seed of unlimited potential, and as you advance by growing, a nonlocal, yet all-pervasive intelligence steps in to orchestrate synchronistic events. As long as you view yourself through a lens confined to a reality in the physical domain, your progress will be limited. Therefore, you must determine your highest purpose, vision, and goals. This book is designed to help you discover them. As in my case, your discovery may include the realization that your purpose had been with you all along.

An all-pervasive pure intelligence works in a nonlinear fashion and is ready to serve you. This applies whether you seek positive or negative goals and limited or unlimited success. For example, if your mind is fixed on the thought of being hopelessly trapped, your goal becomes becoming hopelessly trapped in the physical domain. As a result, synchronicity will start orchestrating events to accommodate your goal. And, the more attention you pay to it, the more help you get toward creating negative experiences until you are hopelessly trapped. Using a commonly used psychological term, you have created a self-fulfilling prophecy.

Trusting Others According to Their Nature

Seeking unlimited success in an area of your choice, you must have trusting relationships with others. That starts by trusting yourself first, which becomes the basis for trusting others according to their nature. Each person has unique strengths and limitations that reveal who they are. Our greatest problem comes when we doubt ourselves and then blindly trust others for qualities they do not have. You must accept what you perceive and assume the responsibility to make your relationships work.

For example, if you lend money to a good friend who has no means of paying it back, but give them a deadline, you show poor judgment. Your relationship with that person will not end well because of your unrealistic expectations. Instead, you must focus on trusting yourself by acknowledging the reality of your friend's situation. Then you have two choices: give the money without strings attached; or say that you have no money to give. Chances are that whatever you decide, you will stay friends.

Unconditional Positive Regard

Beware of the term unconditional love. It is highly subjective, utterly confusing and loaded with unrealistic expectations for both the giver and receiver. There are many interpretations of love, and if things do not go as expected, we might give up the blurry concept altogether and become cynical. The phrase, "If you want unconditional love, get a dog," is an example of that. A more practical term is Carl Roger's unconditional positive regard.[16] The term stands for basic acceptance and support of someone regardless of what they do. In that sense, acceptance does not necessarily equal approval but acknowledges the reality of a situation and the right of others to make their own decisions. By respecting others' rights to personal autonomy—even if their values do not jive with yours—unconditional positive regard provides the foundation for mutually supportive and potentially transformative relationships.

When you grasp that you are the seed of unlimited potential, use sound judgment to trust others according to their nature, and practice unconditional positive regard in all of your relationships, then you have gained an edge; you are perfectively positioned to rise above your previously perceived limitations.

After introducing "The AOVIA Principle: A Path of Unlimited Potential" as a solution to the problem of "The Pain of Feeling Stuck," I will present "Step #1: Ask What Type of Success You Want" in the next chapter. But first, I provide you with another "Dare to Imagine" exercise you can use to process important points from this one and a "Reader's Notes" page to capture your Aha! moments.

Dare to Imagine:

- Thriving on a path of unlimited potential.
- Information coming from areas beyond ordinary consciousness governing you.
- Your sub- and unconscious mind using language coded in signs, symbols, emotions, images, or archetypes.
- Learning to decode the language of your mind beyond ordinary consciousness.
- Liberating yourself from distorted thinking and getting empowered with effective coping strategies.
- A nonlocal but all-pervasive intelligence arranging synchronistic events for you to reach personal goals.
- The AOVIA Principle as a guide on a path of unlimited potential.
- Being the seed of unlimited potential.
- Trusting others according to their nature.
- Treating others with unconditional positive regard.

Margrit Goodhand

Reader's Notes:

CHAPTER THREE

STEP #1: ASK WHAT TYPE OF SUCCESS YOU WANT

*He who asks a question is a fool for five minutes;
he who does not ask a question remains a fool forever.*
~ Chinese Proverb

When implementing the first step of the AOVIA Principle, you must ask yourself what type of success you want. In my case, I discovered my purpose after answering four specific questions. There are many possible answers to these questions and, prompted by my existential crisis, I tried several. In medicine, a crisis presents a turning point of a disease with either death or recovery as the two possible outcomes. I was determined to recover, and after much brainstorming as to possible answers, I chose the ones that led to the emergence of my highest vision and core value, with the latter being my innate fundamental driving force.

The Aovia Principle

When you answer these questions, you also have the opportunity to discover your guiding vision and core value. They will lead you on a path of unlimited potential within your belief system while transcending its barriers. Examples of core values are integrity, service, social justice, the inherent value of persons, the importance of relationships, authenticity, optimism, courage, respect, etc. If needed, you might want to do some research in that area to get a more comprehensive list and see what most strongly resonates with you.

The Four Questions with My Answers:

1. Who am I?

I am a licensed clinical social worker.

2. What do I want to do?

I want to help others feel better. I do that by rekindling their hope and eliciting their motivation using therapy, advocacy, and writing.

3. Who needs or wants what I do?

People who want to feel better about themselves and their lives.

4. How will they benefit?

They benefit by feeling better.

My Vision:

Unlimited success through helping others feel better by rekindling their hope and eliciting internal motivation using therapy, advocacy, and writing.

My Core Value:

Compassion.

The Four Questions for Your Answers:

1. Who am I?

2. What do I want to do?

3. Who needs or wants what I do?

4. How will they benefit from it?

Your Vision:

Unlimited success through ….

Your Core Value:

Using the above method, you are working towards discovering a purpose greater than yourself along with your personal guiding vision and core value. That vision is your overarching main goal or destination, with your core value driving you. For example, having identified my purpose, my overall goal or guiding vision crystalized as "unlimited success helping others to feel better by rekindling their hope and eliciting internal motivation using therapy, advocacy, and writing." And the one word distinctively describing my core value is "compassion."

Engaging in the above work will help you stay on course with what is really important: your inner work and character development on a path of unlimited potential toward your destiny. Staying on course does not preclude the tweaking of your initial answers. I did this several times until my answers were a good fit. And once on your course, you may need to develop new skills as needed. As for me, little did I know that several of my clients are double amputees, some are near death, and most of them have post-traumatic stress disorder. Suffering from such conditions, they not only seek practical support but also search for deeper meaning for transcending the boundaries of the purely physical domain.

While our Western youth-oriented culture promotes ageism as a form of discrimination against seniors, age does not have to be a barrier to a path of unlimited potential. You can define your own success. One of my clients, with the fictitious name of Helena, had done just that. She was 88 years old, lived in an assisted living facility, had numerous medical problems, and was bound to a wheelchair. I will never forget the day I walked into Helena's room. On her dresser was a huge sign with butterflies and the words "Peace Be with You" as a greeting for everyone who entered.

During our first meeting, Helena was resting on her bed and introduced herself as a missionary. At first, I was skeptical. But then I witnessed that despite her condition, she was the person who brought a cheerful light to others in the dining room by greeting them first, using their first names, and throwing around kindness like candy. Helena was also a writer of letters. What really astounded me was that she had a pen pal, a 35-year-old man serving a life sentence in a California prison with whom she had developed a surrogate grandmother/grandson relationship through their regular correspondence. Sometimes, when her arthritis bothered her too much to use a pen, she asked the staff for help. They gladly assisted because she was such a pleasure to be around. Helena, despite her age and physical limitations, was an example of actively moving towards her vision as a missionary of love.

Many public figures are seniors who have hugely impacted others. Three individuals who caught my attention are the current Dalai Lama Tenzin Gyatso, poet and activist Maya Angelou, and American researcher and inspirational management speaker Jim Collins. All three are prolific authors who have made the world a better place and continue to inspire countless individuals around the globe. Tenzin Gyatso was born in 1935 and is 85 years old at the date of this writing. As the 14th Dalai Lama, he is the current spiritual leader of Tibetan Buddhism. He fled the communist regime in 1959, lives in exile in India, and is universally loved and admired.[17] While Dalai Lamas are viewed as reincarnations of previous ones, he shares but transcends that belief with the following words:

"There is no need for temples, no need for complicated philosophies. My brain and heart are my temples; my philosophy is kindness."[18]

Incidentally, while reincarnation has been part of the philosophy of Buddhism, Hinduism, and Judaism—the latter of which describes it as gilgul—it's not surprising that it also had been a fundamental dogma in early Christianity until AD 553.[19] The Dalai Lama has worked closely with Western neuroscientists who study the positive effects of meditation on the brain. He has made several visits to Stanford University's Center for Compassion and Altruism Research and Education (CCARE) to assist with meditation related research and became a benefactor to the center. [20]Further, he practices an ascetic but active lifestyle by rising at 3:00 AM, eating no solid foods after 12:00 PM, meditating about three hours a day, and going to bed at 7:00 PM.[21,22]

While few of us may rise to such a disciplined lifestyle, we can learn some things from the Dalai Lama that optimize our chances of well-being. That includes practicing meditation. If you are completely unfamiliar with meditation, you will find two brief but effective scripts in Chapter Four to get you started. They a basic breath meditation and a body scan meditation. To learn more advanced techniques, I recommend that you find a teacher.

Our brains emanate frequencies called hertz that are measurable. The chart in Table One is based on electroencephalogram (EEG) results that illustrate the depth of mind and functioning within these frequencies. Our everyday functioning occurs in beta, the gateway to the subconscious mind is alpha, the subconscious mind is theta, and the unconscious mind is delta. The fastest brainwave activity occurs in gamma, for only brief moments, promoting the sharpest focus of mind. To be in gamma is sometimes described as the synthesizing of all of the senses, mental processing, and perception.[23,24]

Table 1: Brainwaves and Their Functioning

BRAINWAVES	Freq Hz	DEPTH OF MIND AND FUNCTIONING
BETA	13-39	**Conscious Mind** – day-to-day activity, busy thinking, active concentration, active processing, arousal, cognition
ALPHA	7-13	**Gateway to Subconscious Mind** – in between sleep and waking, light meditation state, calm relaxed yet alert, in the flow state
THETA	4-7	**Subconscious Mind** – deep meditation/relaxation, REM sleep, deeper in the flow state
DELTA	< 4	**Unconscious Mind** - deep dreamless sleep, loss of body awareness, healing, regeneration
GAMMA	40	**Focused Mind** – includes perception, problem solving, consciousness, synthesis of all activity

Poet and activist Maya Angelou, my second example, lived from 1928 until 2014. She continues to deeply inspire others through her books. Growing up in the segregated South,

Maya's beliefs gave her the wings to overcome parental abandonment, great poverty, childhood rape, and even working in the sex trade. She found her voice through poetry and the library and eventually became a Pulitzer Prize winner. At age 60, this senior rose from being one of the most banned authors in the United States for her autobiography *I Know Why the Caged Bird Sings* to becoming one of the most influential voices of the 20th century.[25]

Maya's poem *Still I Rise* shows an indomitable faith that transcends all duality as best expressed during an interview with Oprah Winfrey that "God is all," "soul is spirit that longs for all," that she lives in "all now," and will "return to all" when she dies.[26] Maya's life is a perfect example of how the subconscious mind overcame limited reasoning with belief. This is possible because the subconscious does not differentiate between reality and imagination but primarily seeks to maintain the conceptual self. As such, it cannot hold invalidated beliefs because it is committed to remaining congruent. This is helpful information for anyone intending to rise above their limitations.

My third example, Jim Collins, was born January 25, 1958. At 62 years old, he is best known as a management consultant, inspirational speaker, and author of transformational books. In his book *Good to Great,* Collins introduces his Level 5 leadership concept, based on empirical findings that the most effective leaders strive to serve others as opposed to taking control. With that concept, he invalidated old models of hierarchy based on position. Instead of big charismatic personalities, he describes the greatest leaders often presenting as humble and even shy while also demonstrating an indomitable will for an organization to succeed.[27]

In his foreword to *The Highest Goal* by Michal Ray, Jim talks about almost quitting after attending the first class of a "creativity in business" elective at Stanford. Instead of promises that he would discover his essence within ten weeks, Jim wanted practical methods and techniques. His wife talked him into staying put, and, as a result, he learned how to create room for the life-changing experience of discovering his unique path. An avid rock climber, he compared that path to persevering at the edge, and, instead of using a numbers kit to color within lines, creating a masterpiece of one's life, with the only guiding frame of reference being the highest goal.[28]

In order to assist you with discovering your unique path, please take some time to brainstorm the following questions:

Three Questions for Brainstorming

1. What do you feel passionate about?

2. Are you receptive to a higher purpose?

3. How do you sustain yourself now?

As you continue to read, be prepared to receive more insights related to your passion, purpose, and sustaining yourself. Tweak your answers as you receive new insights that promote recreating yourself. Learning from others is necessary, but settling for the status quo is no longer an option, no matter your age. Instead, aim for making your life a masterpiece!

Potential Barriers to Unlimited Success

More important than adding to your cup is keeping it empty, not only during meditation but in general. Only then are you in a position to receive by allowing synchronistic events to enter your life. Emptying your cup is a prerequisite to receiving and includes eliminating potential barriers. Common barriers are related to fear of failure or success, relationship conflict, problems with boundaries, and ineffective communication. The good news is that by beginning to eliminate your potential barriers, you are on your way. Practicing self-esteem during that process is crucial because it will allow you to move forward—despite struggling with imperfections. Self-esteem is evidenced by the way you value your thoughts, feelings, and actions. It should never be confused with self-confidence that, while also important, is task related.

Fear of Failure or Success and Prejudice

Research indicates that either fear of failure or success can prevent someone from moving forward. These fears are related to learned helplessness, a concept that psychologist Martin Seligman demonstrated during experiments with dogs. Due to classical conditioning, the dogs no longer try to escape electric shocks in an open crate after previously learning to associate the ringing of a bell with subsequently being shocked.[29] Related to learned helplessness is the crippling imposter syndrome when affected individuals question the validity of their success and fear of being exposed as a fraud.[30]

Another problem grounded in fear is holding on to prejudices against others because we perceive them to be different from us. Getting on a path of unlimited potential does not preclude the possibility of financial success. Either prejudice or envy—or a toxic combination of both —may lead you to project your shadow onto others by questioning the validity of their successes. Compare your current thoughts about the Dalai Lama with your thoughts *after* learning that his net worth is approximately $150,000,000.[31] Given such information, is your mind leading you to negative judgments, disregarding all the good he has achieved? Does it matter that the Dalai Lama does not keep a penny for himself? Can you imagine that the more resources you have, the more you can help others?

Relationship Conflict

Do you have unresolved relationship issues and believe that conflict is wrong? We crave being part of our families' protective bubbles, extended families, and the larger meta and mega communities. On the one hand, our relationships with others can be beneficial; on the other hand, we can get hopelessly entangled in their messiness. The first place you learn about relationships is in your own family. Do you view conflict as an opportunity to grow, or do you run from it? Were you allowed to disagree with your parents? Have you learned to negotiate your needs in relationships and create win/win situations? Or are you stuck in win/lose or lose/lose dynamics? You might have to let go of faulty learning, accept that conflict is part of life, and learn to practice unconditional positive regard when dealing with others, a concept previously explored in Chapter Two.

Problems with Boundaries

Another term for boundaries is limits. Healthy boundaries are semipermeable and serve to maintain safety while also promoting mutually beneficial exchanges, similar to how our cells operate. Do you have difficulty with setting your own or respecting others' boundaries? If you let others overstep your physical, emotional, mental, or spiritual boundaries, it can damage not only you but also others who have to deal with the ripple effects. Do you have healthy boundaries for mutually satisfying relationships? If not, you may have experienced early boundary violations and—as a result—learned to perpetuate them, let others take advantage of you, or build walls to isolate. If any of these apply, you may want to seek the assistance of a trauma counselor who can assist you with making needed personal adjustments.

Communication Barriers

As the foundation of trust, honesty is the prerequisite for relationships to work. According to Albert Mehrabian's study, only 7% of meaning is communicated through words, 38% through voice and tone, and 55% through body language.[32] During a human resources investigation, one of my supervisees repeatedly denied that a particular male client was living at her apartment, which was against company policy. Because she was a high performer, I desperately wanted to believe her. Yet, after paying attention to her body language, I noticed that she nodded her head up and down when saying no, contradicting herself. She also held a hand over her mouth while speaking as if to keep the truth inside. Later, the client's probation officer confirmed she had been lying because the officer had delivered a subpoena to the male at their common residence. When communicating with others, be aware that words alone are usually not telling the entire story.

After reading this chapter, have you been able to answer what type of success you want? If not, you might want to return to asking yourself the following questions: Who am I? What do I want to do? Who needs or wants what I do? How will they benefit from it? Based on the answers, did you discover your vision and core value? You must grasp that you are the seed of unlimited success, and that everything you have experienced so far can be of use, despite—and even because—of difficult times. Looking for clues from your childhood, you might even discover the source of your internal motivation there—like I did by imagining myself in the roles of therapist and writer at the age of seven.

According to Leonard Cohen's *Anthem*: "There is a crack in everything. That's how the light gets in."[33] His message is that because of our imperfections our unlimited potential is available with the aid of an all-pervasive intelligence guiding us. Is it possible for you to grasp that you can thrive precisely because of your limitations? If you have read this book so far, perhaps you can ….

After introducing "Step #1: Ask What Type of Success You Want" in this chapter, I will present "Step #2: Observe

Who You Are" in the next one. But first, I provide you with another "Dare to Imagine" exercise you can use to process important points from this chapter and a "Reader's Notes" page to capture your Aha! moments.

Dare to Imagine:

- The type of success you want becoming your guiding vision toward unlimited potential.
- A path of unlimited potential unrestricted by age.
- Overcoming limiting beliefs because your subconscious does not differentiate between reality and imagination.
- Letting your life evolve as a masterpiece instead of following paint by numbers instructions.
- Getting in a receiving mode by emptying your cup so it can be filled with something new.
- Overcoming barriers such as your fear of failure or success, prejudice, envy, relationship conflict, boundary problems, or ineffective communication.
- Thriving not only despite but *because* of your limitations.

Margrit Goodhand

Reader's Notes:

CHAPTER FOUR

STEP #2: OBSERVE WHO YOU ARE

The key to growth is the introduction of higher dimensions of consciousness into our awareness.
~Lao Tzu

In order to implement the second step of the AOVIA Principle, you must engage in self-observation as experience. As in the above quote by Lao Tzu, this allows for the introduction of the higher dimensions of consciousness to enter your awareness.[34] Self-observation manifests as practicing awareness of the interactions between you and your given environment. An easy technique to begin that process is to learn a basic breath meditation.

To practice a basic breath meditation, the only preparation needed is to set aside fifteen minutes and get yourself in a comfortable position by sitting or lying down. There is no need to force a particular breathing pattern. As you engage in this brief meditation, your breath will regulate itself when you automatically enter the alpha state of mind. This is a relaxed yet alert state, in between sleeping and waking, and the gateway to your subconscious. It also is the beginning of accessing the 95% of your mind not ordinarily used during day-to-day functioning.

Basic Breath Meditation

1. Get in a comfortable position that does not constrict any part of your body. Either sitting up or lying down is fine unless you have been trained to assume a formal meditation posture.

2. Close your eyes and take a deep breath. Observe how that breath enters your nose, how it fills your lungs and belly, how it moves back up, and how it leaves through your mouth.

3. Observe your breath. Witness how it enters your nose, how it fills your lungs and belly, how it moves back up, and how it leaves through your mouth. You do not have to control your breath because it will regulate itself.

4. Again, observe your breath. Fully experience how it enters your nose, how it fills your lungs and belly, how it moves back up, and how it leaves through your mouth. Do not fight any distractions such as your own thoughts or background noises. Let them be and focus on experiencing your breath.

5. Continue to observe and experience your breathing until you enter a light meditation state in alpha, the gateway to your subconscious.

6. After about fifteen minutes, open your eyes, get up, and attend to business as usual while enjoying a feeling of wellness and relaxation.

At this point, I want to remind you that this book is not about entering a scientific debate or escaping to a blind belief system. Rather, it is about sharing a systematic way to liberate yourself from the pain of feeling stuck, the suffering of burn-out, or lacking a clear purpose for your life. Nevertheless, it is helpful to present relevant scientific views as background information.

While scientists have been unable to exactly identify what consciousness is, there appear to be two camps. Classical physicists regard consciousness as a deterministic part of physicality and functioning of the brain. Social scientists, such as Alexander Wendt, promote Dr. Alexander Wendt have begun to view consciousness as primal experience through a lens of macroscopic quantum mind theories where people are viewed as wavelike functions and non-deterministic.[35]

Wendt is known for defending the quantum consciousness hypothesis against the classical approach and is concerned with the study of the nature of social reality. In his groundbreaking book *Quantum Mind and Social Science*, he proposes that consciousness is a macroscopic quantum mechanical phenomenon, and that people are literally quantum systems or waves of potentialities. Wendt's theory allows for making sense of phenomena such as intentional behaviors, free will, teleological reasoning, and even our ability to change the past. [36] This promotes the idea of a dynamic interaction between consciousness as primal experience and observation as awareness practice when implementing the AOVIA principle.

Dr. Peter Fenwick is a neuropsychiatrist and neurophysiologist known for his research on patients near death or with clinical death experiences. His work also challenges the assumption that the brain produces consciousness as part of its metabolism. He argues that the brain is a filter for consciousness and that it operates through interactive properties. He compares this to the functioning of universe with invisible dark matter and gravitational forces rotating entities of the entire universe.[37]

If consciousness is a macroscopic quantum mechanical phenomenon, then practicing mindfulness can link to consciousness as experience and create new opportunities by bridging a gap to a field of pure potential. Mindfulness as awareness practice focuses your attention, allows you to be receptive, and lets you to benefit from the impact of measurable brainwaves beyond the current reality of beta. At alpha you are at the gateway to your subconscious mind. It is where you begin connecting to realities that operate beyond your ordinary five senses but on behalf of your intent—with intent based on desire.

It is helpful to view matter, mind, and spirit as distinct but overlapping levels of existence. Perhaps, a helpful analogy is a Russian doll set where smaller dolls are contained in successively larger ones, and the largest one is in an environment not limited by doll configuration. Deepak Chopra clarifies this as: A) a three-dimensional physical domain with solid matter and linear time; B) a quantum domain with energy and information as a place for our minds, thoughts, and self-concept; and C) a virtual or nonlocal domain with energy and unlimited potential as the source of consciousness and intelligence.[38]

The nonlocal domain is a field of pure potential where intelligence as a governing dynamic seems to be the organizing force behind all things that happen in the other domains. Beyond the reach of space and time, an unlimited supply of consciousness and energy arises from that field of pure potential and weaves through the entire world of human experience in a nonlinear manner by orchestrating meaningful coincidences. Jung coined the term "synchronicity" for these meaningful coincidences that arrange desired outcomes.[39]

The purpose of synchronicity is to create the conditions for your intent to work itself into the present. Becoming mindful of these conditions can be compared to turning on a flashlight after viewing the environment in candlelight or taking off limiting blinders. As a result, you are in a position to familiarize yourself with new realities about yourself, others, and the environment that you had previously been unaware of. Incidentally, this allows you access to a brand-new range of relationships and opportunities.

In my case, when a synchronistic event sparked my memory of a significant episode from childhood, it began a process of changing my past, present, and future. It changed my personal past because of a newly emerging paradigm as the background of my life. Further, it is changing Germany's historical past because the gaps in its postwar history are currently filled with information gained from citizen research yielding information that has already been validated. Moreover, it changed my present by introducing ever-evolving opportunities as an independent social work contractor and writer/author. The latter includes having been asked to translate a documentary in book form about the Verschickungskinder. Finally, it changed the potentiality of my future based on an already changed past and present.

Specific methods of practicing self-awareness that impact areas beyond ordinary consciousness include meditation, journaling, neurofeedback, brainwave entrainment, and other forms of visualization as presented in Chapter Five. All these methods aim to balance brain states of hyper- or under arousal and enhance the chances of optimal functioning. My recommendation is to start with journaling and the two previously presented meditations. After you have incorporated these disciplines into your life, you can proceed to more advanced meditation techniques or try some of the other methods I mentioned. At that point, you will also benefit from finding a teacher who can help you navigate the unfamiliar territory that you are trying to explore.

By becoming receptive to your deeper mind states, you will enjoy higher levels of creativity such as invention or even creation. That is because alpha and theta are the states of mind most associated with self-programming without the constraints of the logical mind. We know that children spend much time in theta where they seem to effortlessly learn new skills by play-acting. Artists, athletes, and anyone who attempts to integrate an idea with physical application does the same. Theta is the zone beyond focus that allows for a complete melting of physical reality and imagination.[40] In this state, you have the potential to remove epigenetic blockages impacting the blueprint of DNA. In other words, you can break the chains of blindly following ancestral patterns by first recognizing them and then develop calculated interventions. The latter might include stress management, dietary modifications, and therapy.

Part of self-observation as experience is creating the receptivity for the desired flow of energy and information coming from the domains undergirding your day-to-day consciousness. Let me share with you an example of how—based on psychoanalytic information—I was able to interpret a vivid dream occurring in theta, catching it in alpha, and analyzing it in beta so I could benefit from an alignment of my internal creativity and power in the present. Before you start working with your subconscious, you must accept your psychological shadow as an inseparable part of your mental activity—just like your physical shadow reflects your body movements.

It is crucial that you feel safe in the knowledge that your subconscious can be your best friend by acting as a mirror. If you have been diagnosed with a psychotic disorder or suffer from excessive neurotic guilt and shame, do not attempt your own dream interpretation. In that case, seek the assistance of a skilled therapist first who can help you in that area.

My Dream

In my dream, I looked through an office window and saw a huge black bull roaming in a meadow while grazing, occasionally stomping its feet, and wagging its tail to ward off flies. When it was gone, my friend Renate and I stepped outside for a pleasant walk. The weather was comfortably warm, and the sun was flickering through the leaves of trees along our path. To the left there was a meadow and to the right a jungle. Suddenly, the animal appeared again in the meadow. It seemed preoccupied with freely roaming and feeding. My main feeling was anxiety because the animal's movements seemed unpredictable.

When the animal was out of sight again, Renate and I turned around and headed back to the building by avoiding the meadow and guiding one another on where to go. To the left, was an uphill path between trees where a mob of kangaroos were busy posturing and kicking. To the right, there was a religious compound demarcated by a boundary of loose stones. When we turned around, the compound was on the left and guarded by a stern looking female with a head covering. Renate warned me, "You better watch her." Once back in the building, I occasionally saw the bull from the window and told Renate the animal was so strong that if it really wanted, it could force itself inside by breaking the walls.

My Interpretation

During deep, dreamless sleep in delta, our mind and body heal on sub-molecular levels along with the information that was filed away in theta during dreams. If something needs further attention, a dream shows up as unfinished business upon awakening in alpha, as in my case. If we anticipate something, it can also show up as a prophetic dream, allowing us glimpses into the future. That is similar to computer algorithms collecting and analyzing data about how we have handled our finances in order to predict our future purchasing patterns.

Paying attention to the main feeling of a dream is important as well as to the knowledge that every creature, landscape, and object in a dream represents a facet of the dreamer that is coded as signs, symbols, or images that include archetypes. My first step for interpreting the dream was preparing the groundwork. My main feeling had been anxiety at the sight of the huge animal with some confusion as to whether it was an ox or bull, until the term aurochs clicked in my mind. That settled the issue because aurochs applies to both the female and male species as the precursors of domestic cattle.[41] Further, my mind created an association between what seemed to be huge cattle grazing in a soccer field near our house, and the cattle appearing to be smaller as I grew in size.

The encounter with the aurochs in my dream could have been terrifying. Yet, despite my anxiety, I had sensed that it was not after me. It was simply roaming and feeding in its natural pasture. Both bull and ox are ancient archetypes representing powerful forces of regeneration and for labor that have historically been channeled in the service of civilization. Following psychoanalytic thought, everything in a dream represents an aspect of the dreamer. Therefore, the drive of the aurochs is within me. While my physical expression is female, it is also complemented by an inner animus or male, with the aurochs representing both.

The message was that I have a massive source of internal power to generate new life and get any job done. My anxiety was related to feeling separate from that power and blocking my potential. Renate was my real-life childhood friend whom I met at age five when walking around the perimeter of a soccer field carrying one of my mother's small black purses and looking for a friend to play with. Carrying that purse, I role-played to be older than I was to get the courage to go out into the world. The walk on the sunny path in the dream triggered happy memories of Renate and I walking on a similar path as children in nearby woods, picking wild cherries and flowers.

The head covering of the woman guarding the religious compound represented an ancient religious tradition for females, including the ones in my family. It also represented the historical protective, yet also oppressive, forces that I had "to watch out for" by learning to navigate my own needs while growing up. The woman's face had been stern, not allowing a genuine relationship with me. During past problems, as in the dream, my friend and I promoted safety for each other when faced with trouble. Without acceptance of my shadow side, I would have lacked the insight that I was dealing with epigenetic material coming from my female lineage.

The sight of kangaroos puzzled me at first, but then I remembered that their offspring develop in their mothers' protective pouches where they stay for a long time to be nourished upon demand. This offered the paradigm of keeping my creative projects close and protected during my embryonic awareness until their completion. That safekeeping included not only my natural offspring but also my creative projects, including writing this book.

Further, the kangaroos kicking back and forth at each other in a group reminded me of playing competitive soccer with the boys until I was excluded from such games based on my gender, which was painful. It also reminded me of my weekly writers' group where everyone, including me, has creative projects in their laptop folders (pouches), kicking back and forth feedback that is constructive but can also be challenging.

In my current reality, my mother's purse can hold only a fraction of my adult power. After all, I am a clinical social worker who holds an office for which I have trained and hold credentials. It is notable that in my dream, Renate and I had found safety in the building with our offices. As a result of my dream analysis in beta, I decided that I would take enjoyable walks more often, occasionally stomp my feet in the field of clinical social work, swat all bothersome thoughts away with an imaginary tail, and continue to attend my writers' group—with all of it serving to nurture my creativity.

If you are interested in dream interpretation, you can catch your dreams upon awakening when your mind is in alpha, the gateway to your subconsciousness as shown in Table 1. Further, it helps to record your dreams upon awakening by keeping a journal next to your bed, so you will not forget them and can work with them later. Your capacity of mind increases as the result of your ability to move between brain waves and experiencing different mind states. Anyone who is motivated to learn advanced meditation or dream interpretation is bound to eventually find a teacher familiar with such techniques. Online training may be an option as long as you identify someone as credible.

When compared to a control group with members interested but having no experience in meditation, Buddhist yogis' brain activity with EEGs and fEEGs (a 3D video of brain activity) showed activity of superior mental dexterity as it pertains to moving from one brain state to another, a skill acquired during 15-40 years of meditation several times a day. Further, the yogis showed significantly elevated gamma oscillations when compared to members of a control group. Gamma waves occur during very brief moments of synthesis when different brain regions fire together in harmony. It is the envied state of complete clarity, problem solving, and consciousness—accompanied by feelings of immense compassion as a way of being.[42]

Finally, you might choose hypnotherapy, neurofeedback, or brain entrainment from professional providers. Self-application works if you have an idea that you want to train up from depression or down from anxiety, evoke mental imagery, or achieve deep sleep states for regeneration. While the human brain is a most complex organ as opposed to a muscle, neuroscientists recommend training it like a muscle for optimal performance.[43] For example, you could start with daily practices such as meditation, journaling significant dreams, and engaging in progressive, muscle tension and relaxation.

As you get into a routine, you might want to consider adding additional methods such as advanced meditation techniques, neurofeedback, or brain entrainment through formal instruction. None of these practices should interfere with the ordinary functioning of your life. Instead, they are designed to enrich you with integrated and transformative experiences. In addition to practicing meditation, I journal and interpret my significant dreams. Further, I recently began to experiment with brain entrainment to enhance focus, promote relaxation, and induce sound sleep. This helps me to be at my best, both personally and professionally.

At the time of writing this book, most of my current clients suffer from PTSD. In addition to collaborating with medical professionals for traditional treatment planning, I teach all of them progressive muscle tension and relaxation and at least one mindful meditation technique. I also assist them in interpreting their dreams as an anxiety reducing intervention. As for my clients in the end stages of their lives, I support them in connecting to the deepest layer of self that creates positive meaning in the present while also transcending the physical domain—the latter being entirely dependent on their own belief systems.

At the beginning of this chapter, you already learned the most basic mindful breathing meditation. Going forward, I present a progressive muscle tension and relaxation exercise and a body scan meditation that can further enhance your ability to practice self-awareness. Finally, I introduce the methods and potential benefits of neurofeedback and brain entrainment. If you have been diagnosed with a major mental health disorder such as schizophrenia or bipolar disorder and experience psychotic episodes or paranoia, I do not recommend using any of the above without medical approval.

Progressive Muscle Tension and Relaxation

Have someone you trust read the instructions to you and follow them or record them for later use until you are able to fully memorize all steps without external guidance. This is a highly effective stress management tool I use personally as well as with clients who have no specific interest in meditation. Additionally, it can be used during the induction phase of hypnosis.

1. Lie down on a flat surface or sit down in a chair. Relax all of your limbs.

2. Close your eyes, take a deep breath in, and then breathe out.

3. Take a deep breath, pull your feet (not legs) toward your head, and keep them contracted for several seconds. Now breathe out and relax your feet.

4. Take a deep breath, tighten your calves, and keep them contracted for a few seconds. Now breathe out and relax your calves.

5. Take a deep breath, tighten your thighs, and keep them contracted for a few seconds. Now breathe out and relax your thighs.

6. Take a deep breath, tighten your buttocks, and keep them contracted for a few seconds. Now breathe out and relax your buttocks.

7. Take a deep breath, make fists with both hands, and keep them contracted for a few seconds. Now breathe out and relax your hands.

8. Take a deep breath, contract your arms, and keep them contracted for a few seconds. Now breathe out and relax your arms.

9. Take a deep breath, contract your shoulders, and keep them contracted for a few seconds. Now breathe out and relax your shoulders.

10. Take a deep breath, contract your chest, and keep it contracted for a couple of seconds. Now breathe out and relax your chest.

11. Take a deep breath, contract your stomach, and keep it contracted for a couple of seconds. Now breathe out and relax your stomach.

12. Take a deep breath, contract your forehead, and keep it contracted for a couple of seconds. Now breathe out and relax your forehead.

13. Take a deep breath, contract your cheeks, and keep them contracted for a couple of seconds. Now breathe out and relax your cheeks.

14. Take a deep breath, contract your chin, and keep it contracted for a couple of seconds. Now breathe out and relax your chin.

15. Take a deep breath, contract your neck muscles, and keep them contracted for a couple of seconds. Now breathe out and relax your neck muscles.

16. Again, take a deep breath and contract all of your muscle groups at the same time. Keep them contracted until you begin to tremble from the tension. Now breathe out and relax all of your muscles.

17. Once more, take a deep breath and again contract all of your muscle groups at the same time. Again, keep them contracted until you to tremble from

the tension. Now breathe out and relax all of your muscles.

18. Open your eyes, slowly breathe in and out, get up, and enjoy the feeling of deep relaxation while going about your ordinary business.

Body Scan Meditation

Have someone you trust read the instructions to you and follow them or record them for later use until you are able to fully memorize all steps without external guidance.

1. Lie down on a flat surface or sit in a chair relaxing all limbs.

2. Close your eyes and take three deep breaths.

3. Now take a deep breath and feel it enter your nose as your nostrils widen.

4. Follow your breath all the way into the bottom of your lungs as you inflate your stomach.

5. Now follow your breath as it leaves your body deflating your stomach and moving out of your lungs and out of your mouth.

6. Continue to breathe in the above manner but shallower until you feel yourself getting into a natural and effortless rhythm.

7. If you get distracted by your own thoughts, do not fight them, simply continue to refocus on your breathing.

8. As you continue to breathe, focus on different parts of your body, and witness any sensations without judgement.

9. Be sure to include scanning your feet, calves, thighs, buttocks, hands, arms, shoulders, back, chest, stomach, forehead, cheeks, chin, and neck. Feel free to scan any other body parts such your eyes, nose, fingers, toes, etc.

10. After completing your body scan, take another three deep breaths.

11. Open your eyes, get up, and enjoy the feeling of relaxation while going about your ordinary business.

Neurofeedback

Neurofeedback is a form of biofeedback and trains higher brain wave functioning. The simplest way to explain biofeedback is taking your temperature or blood pressure. Your body will provide you with feedback on what exactly that temperature is. Neurofeedback provides feedback on neural activity. This is accomplished by placing electrodes on the scalp for measuring and regulating brainwaves.

Designed to assist someone to self-regulate their brain activity, neurofeedback is currently used as a therapeutic tool, for peak performance training, and as an experimental method.[44] Progress is achieved by the process of Skinner's operant conditioning, which makes the probability of a future response dependent on an association with an immediately following consequence. For example, the smooth functioning of a simple film involving butterflies and flowers within an optimal range is the positive reward. Negative feedback is provided by pausing the film when your brainwaves fire at a rate that is not optimal. As a result, your brain, with minimal effort, figures out what it must do to continue with the movie.

In the past, people had to go to a provider for neurofeedback training. Today, home neurofeedback with initial brain mapping and concurrent coaching during the application is available at a fraction of the cost of using an outside neurofeedback lab. You purchase an app, reading headband, and EEG scalp sensor to monitor your brainwaves and your smartphone or tablet sends feedback to you through a video. It yields the same positive effects as years of practicing meditation but works much faster. Every time we learn something new, our brain physically changes with some synapses getting stronger and others getting weaker.

Over time, neurofeedback can help you to improve your brain's functioning, potentially resulting in long lasting positive changes. Several high-end rehabs like the Betty Ford Center in Hazleton, Pennsylvania or HealthCare Connection in Tampa, Florida use neurofeedback therapy. Athletes, celebrities, and other elite performers use it as well to train for optimal performance. These include Tony Robbins, American author, public speaker, and life coach; Kerri Walsh-Jennings, American professional beach volleyball player, three-time Olympic gold medalist, one-time bronze medalist; and Chris Kaman, former German American NBA professional basketball player.[45]

Brain Entrainment

Brain entrainment is any procedure that uses a combination of sound and light to stimulate brain waves toward synchronizing activity. Just like during regular meditation and neurofeedback, it can balance the left and right hemispheres of the brain but much faster than either of the other methods alone or combined. Compared to neurofeedback that teaches skill building, brain entrainment—with your permission—pushes the brain into a given position. The goal is to achieve whole brain synchronization. That opens the door to numerous potential benefits such as less stress, greater success, improved mental health, super creativity, deeper sleep, and easier learning.[46]

Because brain entrainment pushes the brain into a given position, I do not recommend it without medical approval. I recently purchased an app that allows me to connect to a variety of alpha, theta, and delta waves by using my smartphone with earbuds and getting into desired mind states. For example, if unable to sleep, I can listen to delta waves bring me into a deep sleep from which I awake completely refreshed. In order to relax for learning and studying, I can listen to alpha. And in order to problem solve or calm my anxiety, I can listen to theta.

After introducing "Step #2: Observe Who You Are" in this chapter, I will present "Step #3: Visualize Your Desired

Goal" in the next one. But first, I provide you with another "Dare to Imagine" exercise you can use to process important points from this chapter and a "Reader's Notes" page to capture your Aha! moments.

Dare to Imagine:

- Self-observation manifesting as degrees of awareness of the interaction between you and a given environment.
- Consciousness existing inside and outside of your brain as an interactive property of the universe itself.
- The human brain operating on five major types of brainwaves called beta, alpha, theta, delta, and gamma that determine the depth of your mind and its functioning.
- Self-observation as experience creating the receptivity for the desired flow of energy and information coming from your personal subconscious and the collective unconscious areas of the mind.
- Accessing the areas beyond ordinary consciousness by using methods such as journaling, dream interpretation, progressive muscle tension and relaxation, meditation, neurofeedback, or brain entrainment.
- A collective or universal unconscious serving as the governing dynamic underlying the whole world of human experience.
- A nonlocal yet all-encompassing intelligence from a field of pure potentiality orchestrating seemingly unrelated coincidences for you via synchronistic events.

Reader's Notes:

CHAPTER FIVE
∞
STEP #3: VISUALIZE YOUR DESIRED GOAL

Imagination is more important than knowledge. Knowledge is limited. Imagination encircles the world.
~Albert Einstein

In order to implement the third step of the AOVIA Principle, you must imagine your highest purpose. That is looking through the lens of your inner eye and envisioning your deepest desires. There is a difference between imagination and visualization. One could say that imagination is the act of dreaming about the life you want, and visualization is the act of picturing a specific image in your mind which sets in motion the creative process of the unfolding of these desires. Einstein perfectly expressed his idea of imagination in the quote above.[47]

Individuals with developmental or neurological disorders might be unable to imagine tangible and intangible things in their minds. Nevertheless, depending on individual conditions, they might still be able to create tangible visuals in the form of drawing simple illustrations, developing a mind map, or using computer software. Such tangible visualization empowers a person just as visualization in the mind. Generally, visualization as mental imagery is not necessary for memory, imagination, creativity, or having an otherwise successful life.[48]

By now you should have answered the questions designed to assist you discovering your highest purpose as a basis for developing your guiding vision and core value. In case you did not, please return to the previous pages and take some time to complete that work now. This is important because each step builds on a previous one. In order to benefit from your 95% of consciousness below ordinary functioning, you must focus on yourself. Further, you must embrace the idea that ultimately you are 100% responsible for your own happiness.

This applies whether you are single or married, employed or unemployed, have your own company or are retired. If you do not focus on yourself, you will lack the ability to form true partnerships. You will remain stuck by either collapsing into the life of others or let others collapse into yours. As a result, you will create unhealthy dependencies on or for others that ultimately leave everyone feeling miserable. The solution is practicing healthy boundaries that allow for the mutual flow of tangible and intangible resources.

If your focus is doing things for someone at the cost of yourself, you will get trapped in a cat and mouse game of mindlessly acting and reacting, and your codependent world is doomed to ultimately fall apart. The opposite of codependency is narcissism, which is using others as supply to feed an inflated sense of grandiosity or addiction. While codependent and narcissistic personalities attract each other like magnets, subsequent relationships have often traumatic endings. A healthier focus is to generously act in the roles of spouse, partner, friend, co-worker, or employee while also setting and respecting personal boundaries.

Once you have identified a purpose greater than yourself by using your imagination, that purpose becomes your vision or main goal overarching any subsequent goals. When faced with limiting parameters, it helps to step outside an imagined box around your problem that cannot be solved with logical thinking. Once out of the box, you are able to view your problem from a new perspective and solve it with "lateral thinking," a term coined by Edward De Bono.[49] To assist you with conceptualizing that approach, I have provided two examples. The first one is the *Nine Heart Challenge* in Figure 2 and the second one the parable on "Black and White." Both are lessons for solving complex problems outside given parameters.

The Aovia Principle

Nine Heart Challenge

Without taking the pen or pencil of the paper, attempt to connect all nine hearts with four continuous lines.

Figure 2

Refer to the end of this chapter for the solution.

On Black and White
Margrit Goodhand

Sometimes, things are not black and white, although they might be presented that way by someone who plots to take advantage of us when we are vulnerable. In such cases, it is necessary to step "outside the box" in order to avoid a disastrous outcome.

The villagers called him Azazel, the claw. He was a greedy and wealthy banker of unsightly appearance. In order to compensate, he wore the most expensive tailored suits and had impeccably manicured fingernails. Azazel was skilled to put undue pressures on clients who were unable to pay their debts—no matter the cause. Such an unfortunate soul was Eli, the tanned farmer with tattered clothes and rough hands from his strenuous agricultural work who had just lost his wife. He had been unable to pay back a loan for his farming equipment because of her medical bills, and now it was due.

Azazel knew that Eli had a stunningly beautiful daughter named Jewel whom he coveted to possess. While he was smart, he was also unethical and used his poisonous intellect to skillfully deceive others using logic while presenting himself as though he had done the right thing. Further, guarding his reputation as a fair businessman was important to him. That is how he started with Eli:

> You have known for a long time that the deadline for paying your debt to me is today. But I am a fair man and will provide you with three options

to choose from in order to seal your own fate. It will be up to you to choose the best one. These are your options:

1. You must pay your debt in full now.
2. I will report you as delinquent and you will surely end up in prison and lose your farm, which I want to avoid.
3. I will forgive all your debt if you give me your daughter as my wife.

Because Azazel was a crook pretending to be fair, he also attempted to trick Eli into thinking that his daughter had a say in the matter. He picked two small pebbles off the ground, put them inside a bag and, pretending to be generous, he offered:

"I have placed two pebbles in my bag. One is white, the other one is black. If your daughter picks the black one, your debts will be forgiven but she will have to marry me. If she picks the white one, your debts will also be forgiven, and she does not have to marry me."

Reluctantly, Eli agreed and nodded for Jewel to cooperate. Taking her father's cue, she walked over to Azazel. Fortunately, Jewel was an astute girl thinking for herself, a trait she had inherited from her mother. While Azazel had been busy trying to deceive her father, she had seen him picking up two black pebbles. That is why she knew that she was in a lose/lose situation by either going along with his proposal or directly confronting him.

Therefore, Jewel chose the following course of action: She put her hand in the bag and picked a pebble. While taking it out, she pretended to stumble and let it drop to the ground where it quickly disappeared among the other pebbles of various sizes and colors. Then she immediately assumed responsibility for her action by profusely and respectfully apologizing.

"Dear Sir, I am awfully sorry for my clumsiness and dropping the pebble! That was a terrible mistake on my part. But I think I have a solution that will work to make things right: If you just check inside of your bag, your will see what color of pebble is left. And if it is white, I must have picked the black one and will gladly marry you."

Because Azazel did not want to be exposed for the crook he was, he agreed. And, since the pebble in the bag was black, Eli's debt was forgiven, and Jewel did not have to marry him.

#

The above parable is a template for solving complex problems by using lateral thinking.

The black and white pebbles are metaphors for limited choices that are given by someone who wants to take advantage of you. I discovered that trusting my own perceptions is a good basis for developing creative solutions that promote positive outcomes.

The ability to think outside given limitations to solve problems will equip you to overcome great obstacles. That is because you have become teachable by and receptive to pure intelligence generating synchronistic opportunities that assist you on a path. An example from my own life is that I no longer wanted to be a secretary. Instead, I planned to get an undergraduate college degree in Applied Behavioral Science at Penn State before moving on to postgraduate education. In retrospect, I am still amazed that I did not take no for an answer, met all the right people along the way, and ultimately reached my goal—before I had heard anything about lateral thinking.

I was scheduled to take an advanced math test at Penn State Harrisburg on a day that conflicted with my work schedule at Philhaven Behavioral Health; therefore, I could not call off. As an administrative secretary to the director of development, I was expected to accompany him to a golf tournament fundraiser during the time of the test. Being solution oriented, I asked my professor if he could fax the exam to the local branch of the community college where I would take it under the supervision of the librarian in the evening. He replied, "No problem but you have to arrange it." When I asked the librarian, she countered, "Absolutely not, that's not part of my job description." After explaining my dilemma to the dean of the community college, he assured me, "Yes, you can take it here, I will talk to the librarian. Just let her know what time you will be in to take the test." I followed his advice, the librarian watched me take my test, and faxed my completed exam to Penn State. The rest is history.

A major hurdle that I learned to overcome at Philhaven was my fear of falling or abandonment. I signed up for a ropes course offered to employees as part of a team building initiative, and my participation in a trust fall transformed my life. Our instructor demonstrated falling backwards from a 12-foot ladder into the arms of a row of employees standing in pairs face to face, with arms connected in a way that allowed them to bounce upon impact of the body. When done, he asked for a volunteer. I visualized that I could do it by calculating "if they can catch the instructor who is taller and heavier than I am, then they can catch me."

I never forgot the intense feeling of fear as I stood on the ladder right before falling backwards. Although my legs were shaking, I was determined to go through with the trust fall. As our instructor had done previously, I shouted, "Will you catch me?!" "Yes, we will!" came the reply in unison. Upon closing my eyes, I almost fainted while letting myself fall backward from the 12-foot ladder. I safely ended up in the arms of my coworkers, feeling an up and down bounce on my backside. My trust fall experience changed my life because that day I learned to trust myself before anyone else. I saw someone modeling how to succeed, checked with others to verify that they would support me in taking a calculated risk, and, having seen them catch another person before me, it verified their trustworthiness.

After securing a position as psychiatric assistant, I learned progressive muscle tension and relaxation and several mindful meditation techniques to prepare the patients for groups. Further, I completed a dream interpretation workshop at the local Sexual Abuse and Resources Center (SARCC). What I learned during that workshop not only benefited me but also many of my clients over the years. After moving to Florida to start a paid post-graduate internship at HealthCare Connection, I began working with physicians, attorneys, and nurses suffering from substance abuse and co-occurring disorders who were in mandated treatment monitored by their respective licensing boards to avoid the permanent loss of credentials.

At HCC, I was introduced to neurofeedback as complementing traditional therapies and, as all staff, I had the opportunity to use the lab myself. Over the years of working with clients, I refined my dream interpretation techniques as part of my postgraduate experience. Yet, I consider myself far from being unique. I like the analogy of comparing myself to being one pebble among many others of different sizes and colors. There is a time for every season under heaven, and today I am happy to be a writer and therapist that works with mostly seniors, some of whom are double amputees.

For my clients who are near death, I use client-centered and supportive techniques in addition to other therapies. Often, they share experiences with me that they will not disclose to anyone else. What they hold most precious during the last phase of their lives, I chose to honor and validate without imposition of my own belief system or opinions. For example, my 82-year old patient with the fictitious name of Anna is longing to be with a comforting white light she once encountered, has brief visions of relatives that are no longer alive, or senses a presence touching her left arm before something unusual is about to happen. She reported that the last time she sensed that presence, she felt the hair on that arm standing up while watching TV.

Later that afternoon, Anna got a phone call from her daughter, an opioid addict, telling her that she was homeless again and wanted to borrow her van for a couple of days. Anna had recently lost her entire life savings in an effort to save her daughter by paying her debts, which of course was to no avail. She believed that she had been forewarned by a premonition and asked for my assistance in teaching her to set firm boundaries and linking the daughter to a treatment center. Consequently, I prepared Anna for the next encounter with her daughter by engaging her in the visualization technique of role-play. This helped with easing her into an effective course of action.

There are several methods of visualization. In this book, I am introducing you to the following four:

1. Role-Play
2. Creating Goal Pictures
3. Positive Affirmations
4. Hypnotherapy/Hypnosis

Role-Play

Role-play is a powerful technique to prepare for the real thing. It promotes effortless learning and a complete melting of physical reality and imagination in theta. Children, artists, and athletes spend a lot of time acting "as if." Long before using any formal method of visualization, I practiced it informally, as all children do. When imagining myself in the roles of therapist and writer age seven, I also engaged in role-play by typing imaginary books on an old typewriter without paper and the A-key missing.

Visualization is mostly effective when cycling between the alpha and theta states of mind that are associated with self-programming without the constraints of the logical mind. I still remember the first time I consciously role-played; it was in preparation to ask for a pay raise the next day. I was at a friend's house where I practiced what I planned to say while my friend pretended to be my boss. She helped me to tweak the script in between sunbathing and jumping in the pool. Scared to actually follow through, I mustered the courage, and, as a result got a surprising 13% raise.

The greatest enemy to role-play is the rational mind that can analyze away any possibility of achieving success. An example was my 85-year old client with the fictitious name of Eileen. Eileen was well-educated, had a Ph.D., and resided in an independent senior living community. She struggled with hopelessness because her adult children did not call or visit her more often than she wanted. Yet, when sporadically reaching out to her, she had the habit of contaminating the present with complaints like, "I have not heard from you for four weeks. What are you doing that is more important than visiting your mother? Why don't you call or come see me more often?" She also refused to participate in any social activities in her community complaining that the other residents were "too different" instead of looking for commonalities.

My first assignment for Eileen was to imagine what a satisfying relationship with her children would look like in terms of calls or visits, the setting, body language, and topics of conversation. It also included showing how happy she is when they do call or visit her. She was to practice interacting with them in a way that focuses on the already positive aspects of the relationships, practice being affectionate, and talk about positive memories.

In my experience, most adult children cannot get enough of hearing how cute or mischievous they were as youngsters. They love to hear examples such as "You were my favorite when . . . . I just loved it when . . . . It was too funny when . . . . I was so proud of you when . . . ." I tell my grandson that he is my favorite grandson. Being my only male grandchild, he knows that the favorite part cannot be true. It really does not matter though because he soaks it up like sunshine anyway!

After Eileen was able to imagine herself in a great relationship with her four adult children, we worked on a strategy to establish herself in the rightful role as family matriarch. That included initiating weekly phone calls with all of them and scheduling one to two hour visits every two weeks. She learned asking them for favors like bringing a dessert while offering to make tea and responding to negative comments by confidently rolling with resistance instead of thoughtlessly reacting.

Rolling with resistance is reframing a negative statement to a positive one or just asking questions to keep the conversation going. For example, instead of recoiling from a perceived accusation or snapping back, one might reply with several open-ended questions such as "What makes you say something like that, honey?" "Explain that to me some more, dear child." or "Sunshine, what makes you think that way?" Responding with such phrases and showing genuine interest is effective because eventually the other party gives up because the pushing of buttons is no longer effective.

What better opportunity for all of us to start doing now what we might have failed to do in the past: Practice and act like more affectionate parents instead of waiting for our adult children to read our minds and discouraging them when they do reach out to us.

Creating Goal Pictures

Examples of goal pictures are vision boards, collages, or picture books. All are used for goal planning and success. In the past, I have used vision boards for strategic planning that allows for employee input and participation towards goal setting. Further, I have assigned clients to create collages that present a desired emotional state or other goal within specific contexts. My favorite for personal use is creating goal picture books by compiling visual representations of the goals I want to achieve. I get these from old magazines, catalogs, or even advertising.

The use of the goal picture method allows for an unfolding process of inspiration because it does not have to be completed in one setting. You start with one image and add additional ones to further clarify your goal. When satisfied with one page, you move to the next one. As you set aside a couple of minutes each day to work on or look through your book, the pictures leave imprints in your subconscious and get your creative juices flowing. The fun lies in enjoying the creative process of collecting new images that represent you goal and, over time, actually achieving it.

Pictorial representations are powerful tools to work toward reaching a practical goal or desired emotional state. If unaware, they can also work against you. One of my clients had recurring nightmares about a scary-looking clown. Consequently, she was haunted by flashbacks of their faces during the day. This only started making sense when I discovered that she had a poster of the rock group KISS on the wall behind her bed. No wonder she was dreaming about scary-looking clowns; it was the last thing she saw at night and the first thing in the morning. Be careful what destination picture you hang over your bed unless you want to end up there one day!

Positive Affirmations

Trying to talk yourself into something by only using verbal affirmations is useless and can be counterproductive. My client with the fictitious name of Betty lived in a halfway house for women where I had worked. She had lost control over her drinking after her son's death in a car accident and her subsequent divorce. Betty confided in me that despite all of her good intentions to stop drinking, her cravings for alcohol had worsened—despite telling herself at least five times a day, "I will stop drinking vodka!"

After complimenting Betty on her honorable goal to "stop drinking vodka," I explained that our psyche is built in a way to only hear the last two words (drinking vodka), and that she had actually been conditioning herself five times a day to relapse. I also taught her that an effective affirmation has to be both positive and accompanied by symbolic or written associations that our subconscious understands.

During a subsequent process of brainstorming, Betty came up with, "I can stay sober today!" To strengthen her resolve, she selected an amethyst—an ancient Greek and Roman symbol representing sobriety and spirituality—that created a powerful positive association in her mind. And, instead of continuing to program herself to relapse, she started to reprogram herself to stay "sober today."

Betty practiced her positive affirmation three times a day, with at least one time while standing in the middle of a group of 15 other women. Holding up her amethyst, she shouted, "I can stay sober today!" And the women provided Betty with positive reinforcement by responding, "Yes, you can!" Eventually, Betty reestablished regular contact with her estranged daughter, enrolled in community college, earned her credentials as a lab technician, secured a job at a medical center, and got engaged.

Hypnotherapy/Hypnosis

Hypnotherapy is not stage hypnosis. It is guided hypnosis with the help of a clinical hypnotherapist to help you make desired changes or to regain control over specific areas of your life. Hypnosis was practiced by ancient cultures such as Sumeria, Persia, China, India, Egypt, Greece, and Rome. Often, the sick went to healing places such as dream or sleep temples to be cured. The scientific history of hypnosis in the West began during the 18th century and was the collective brainchild of many well-known physicians.[50]

Today medical hypnosis is used as a tool by physicians, dentists, licensed clinical social workers, psychologists, and other therapists as an adjunct form of treatment for many conditions, including pain management. It is helpful for patients with issues such as depression, anxiety, phobias, substance abuse disorders, smoking cessation, weight loss, low self-esteem, stress management, irritable bowel syndrome, or individuals who just want to improve their focus or confidence.[51]

Hypnotherapy includes returning to earlier periods of life to gain knowledge about troubling events or programming for future success. A structured hypnotherapy session includes a hypnotic induction, deepening, script, and trance termination. The first session also includes a pretalk. I recently learned hypnotherapy, obtained certification, and added it to my therapeutic skills set.

This is my experience of working with Fred, a 50-year-old male who had trouble staying focused on his goals. His distractions came from the environment and intrusive thoughts and feelings. They impeded his ability to move forward and meet deadlines or reach important goals he had set. Fred wanted to try hypnotherapy to complement his traditional psychotherapy.

The Pretalk

A pretalk with Fred before a session allowed time for introductions, building rapport, establishing goals, explaining what is going to happen during the session, and answering questions. It also included clarifying that he will be fully aware during the session and that remembering anything afterward does not preclude that he was not hypnotized. We established Fred's problem and the corresponding solution, which is the opposite of the problem and agreed on the following:

> The Problem: Because I get distracted, I have difficulty reaching personal goals. I let things get in the way. Because I procrastinate, I feel bad about myself for not doing and getting what I really want.

> The Solution: I will increase focus, so I reach personal goals. I will stay on task, despite distractions in my environment. I will immediately attend to tasks so I can feel good about doing what I really want, which is reaching my goals.

The Hypnotic Induction

Generally, the induction begins with a guided meditation to a beach, an island, the mountains, etc. and might be accompanied by a progressive muscle tension and relaxation exercise until the client is feeling completely at ease. For Fred's induction, I chose a trip to an island with a beautiful, smart, and friendly horse. During the entire session, I use my hypnotic voice with a tone that is pleasant to listen to.

The Deepening

Usually, the deepening is accomplished by using a countdown technique from ten to one while, for example, evoking imagery of the sun setting or walking down a staircase. For Fred's deepening, I chose the imagery of walking down a flight of worn but solid wooden steps. I directed him to focus on a specific point on the wall, his eyes open at ten while breathing in and then closing them at nine while breathing out. I continued that breath and number pattern while suggesting progressive feelings of heaviness and difficulty keeping his eyes open until reaching the number one. At number one, Fred's eyes were closed. That is when I ended the deepening with the following:

> Now that you are completely relaxed, at ease, and secure, you move into a state of mind twice as relaxed. You anticipate freeing yourself from getting distracted, having difficulties reaching personal goals, letting things get in the way of reaching them, and feeling bad about yourself for not doing

and getting what you really want. Instead, you will celebrate your success by increasing your focus and reaching personal goals, staying on task, moving forward despite distractions in your environment, and immediately attending to necessary tasks so you can feel good about doing what you really want, which is reaching your goals.

The Script

The script is where the hypnotherapy is taking place. For Fred, I used an abbreviated progressive muscle tension and relaxation exercise and telling a story that acts like a parable to guide him toward the desired solution of his problem. The story was about a smart horse named Providence running toward its goal. While running, Providence avoided all distractions from the other horses by increasing focus and staying on track until reaching its destination. There are countless scripts for hypnotherapy. These include targeting depression, anxiety, phobias, substance use disorders, smoking cessation, weight loss, stress management, low self-esteem, irritable bowel syndrome, etc. Scripts make heavy use of isometry, analog marking, or metaphors by telling stories that leave imprints on your subconscious mind toward influencing your conscious mind.

Isometry is using imagery to evoke the involvement of the central and autonomic nervous systems to function as if awake (e.g., running and building up stamina). Analog marking facilitates the subconscious to accept a grouping of words hidden within a larger text and perhaps masked as the same sounding word (e.g., knows for nose) that the subconscious does not differentiate. Stories with metaphors act like parables that create templates for desired outcomes.

Toward the end of the script, I foreshadowed the trance termination for Fred. I told him that at the count of three he will view himself in his new way of life, feel happy, be fully conscious and, upon awakening, remember nothing. No requirement to remember anything is needed for hypnotherapy to be effective. Remembering would actually be counterproductive because your analytical mind might explain that you have been reprogrammed.

The Trance Termination

During the trance termination, I ended the session with Fred in my usual way. I spoke a bit louder and faster and said "In a few moments you will return to your waking self. I will now start counting backward from three to one. One: You are beginning to feel awake and happy. Two: You now feel more relaxed and happier than when you first came in. Three: Open your eyes and feel fully awake and incredibly happy now."

While guided by scripts based on my training, I tweak these methods to tailor them to an individual's needs and situation. That is because hypnosis promotes a mental state during which a person utilizes their capacity for self-healing and transformation. A hypnotherapist assists others in dealing with their own challenges by guiding them into an alpha state of mind, while also cycling them into theta where most of the reprogramming takes place. Delta can be used to delve into the deepest issues. For example, prior to the discovery of ether, hypnosis was the major form of sedation used during surgery for blocking the sensation of pain in delta, the same frequency of waves experienced during deep sleep or a coma.[52]

After introducing "Step #3: Visualize Your Desired Goal" in this chapter, I will present "Step #4: Implement Specific Steps Towards Your Goal" in Chapter Six. But first, I provide you with another "Dare to Imagine" exercise you can use to process important points from this one and a "Reader's Notes" page to capture your Aha! moments.

Dare to Imagine:

- Visualizing your highest purpose.
- Being responsible for your own happiness.
- Facing your complex problems.
- Learning to think outside the box.
- Taking calculated risks.
- Learning from others while being yourself.
- Using methods of visualization to manifest goals.
- Benefiting from using methods of visualization such as role-play, creating goal pictures, positive affirmations, and hypnotherapy/hypnosis.

Reader's Notes:

The Aovia Principle

Solution to Nine Heart Challenge

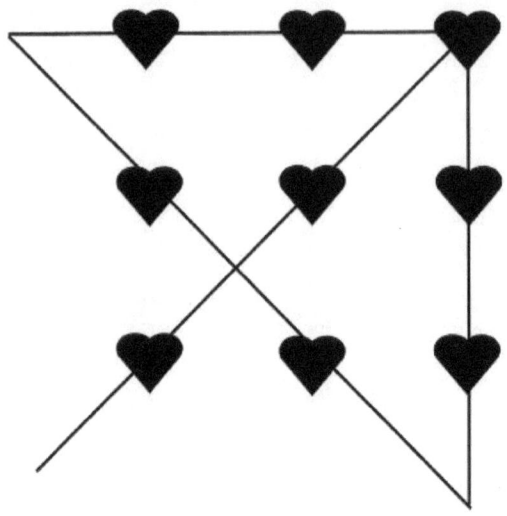

Figure 3

CHAPTER SIX
∞
STEP #4: IMPLEMENT SPECIFIC STEPS TOWARD YOUR GOAL

A journey of a thousand miles begins beneath one's feet.
~Lao Tzu

The more commonly known statement *A journey of a thousand miles begins with one step* is an incorrect translation. Starting with your feet only shows you where you are at a given moment. Research has shown that if people are lost, they walk in circles. The same happens if they are blindfolded. This is because without vision, the brain miscalculates.[53] On the mental plane, you first visualize a goal that ultimately manifests on the physical plane. My friends who are runners know that the most effective running form is looking at the ground 10-20 feet ahead. That not only gives them the advantage of speed but also allows them to see what is coming and avoid falling. During both physical and mental movement, it helps to look ahead by staring at nothing but seeing everything.

The good news is that by now you have already built a solid foundation for further advancement. You did this by completing the work related to *Ask, Observe, and Visualize* during the previous chapters. As a result, you have developed an overall vision that is tied to your highest purpose and identified what type of success you want. Additionally, you have identified your core value. Moreover, you have developed skills of observation as awareness practice. Finally, you have learned about different methods of visualization toward reaching your goals. At this point, you are ready to develop a list with your own goals and objectives. To that end, I have provided you with my own list as an example during the next page. A rather general list, it can give you an idea how to start.

My Goals and Objectives

Goal A: Writing My Book

Objectives:

1. Purchase and keep in stock necessary tools (e.g. paper and cartridges).
2. Purchase Microsoft Office.
3. Complete needed research.
4. Lots of writing and rewriting.
5. Get expert reviews on various subjects.
6. Stay in touch with other writers.
7. Learn to change dots per inch (DPI) for images.
8. Learn to place text or picture box holders.
9. Learn to create a bibliography and end notes in MS Word.
10. Find an editor/s.
11. Find a publisher.
12. Select a book cover.

Goal B: Independent Social Work Contractor

Objectives:

1. Purchase necessary tools (e.g., update computer applications, books, work phone).
2. Create my weekly and monthly schedules.
3. Set limits for the number of my referrals.
4. Stay in touch with other therapists.
5. Complete mandatory continuing education.
6. Renew professional licenses and certifications.
7. Develop new clinical skills (e.g., working with double amputees).
8. Develop new technical skills as the result of COVID-19 (i.e., using a telehealth therapy application).

Your Goals and Objectives

Goal A:

Objectives:

Goal B:
Objectives:

Once I did my own groundwork and discovered my personal vision, there was no stopping me. I wanted no less than unlimited success helping others to feel better by rekindling their hope and eliciting internal motivation using therapy, advocacy, and writing. Guided by the AOVIA Principle, I intuitively knew how to move forward. My path became a quantum experience by providing me numerous opportunities for personal and professional growth as a therapist and writer.

Your definition of unlimited success is a personal one and must be tied to your highest purpose, as was mine. No one can do it for you. On your path you will encounter those who are helpful and those who sabotage your efforts—if you let them. I learned to look at the roots where others come from, what supports their growth, and what holds up their problem. Such roots include but transcend families of origin. Some people are loving and kind, despite having endured the most horrific hardships and become loving parents. Others, despite their good fortune, look at the world through a lens of never-ending cynicism.

When we are not tied down physically, we can either walk toward or away, give or receive, and embrace or reject. The choice is ours and depends on the individual situations. So, what are our roots? As a social worker I am trained in systems theory. When working with others, I look at a what we call PIE (Person in the Environment). I create genograms or ecomaps to assist a person identifying what resources they might already have, what they want to strengthen, let go off, and newly create. This includes relationships. Practicing mindfulness, we can determine the roots that nurture our lives and the life of others.

I find it fascinating how Native American animism precedes but also complements scientific findings of our symbiotic relationship and integration with the ecosystem. According to what Forbes identified as the Native American concept of the "Wemi Tali" (All Where), we are rooted like trees, but our roots come out of our mouth and nose and in that way, connect us to the rest of the world. Even if we lose major body parts, we live as long as we breathe, and everything that we do in life is interactive, including the process of death.[54]

This concept corroborates that all biological processes are interactive mechanisms. We are dependent on green trees and plants to produce the oxygen we get by inhaling and that we cannot live without. In turn, they are dependent on us to exhale the carbon dioxide they need for photosynthesis together with sunlight and water. As interactive living organisms, humans can be energizing or toxic to each other and the rest of the world. Observation as awareness practice can help us to promote overall wellness with breath and all other activity.

Today, ancestry research and genetic testing can be valuable tools to discover the bigger picture of your origin. They have become easily available, and using them, you can learn amazing things about yourself. While some people may think, "Who cares," you should because of the possible adaptations your ancestors had to make in order to survive.

With the ability to follow their migrations, involvement in wars, slavery, the Inquisition, or the Holocaust, you can perceive the footprints or epigenetic changes they might have left you with as a result of famine, poverty, and trauma.

These epigenetic changes determine our phenotypes or observable traits. The stress from environmental pressures results in chemical processes that scientists call methylation or demethylation of alleles and may not only show up in us but also our offspring. While epigenetic processes help us adapt and survive, they might also predispose us to certain conditions that comprise physical, mental health, and social challenges. That can include addiction, depression, anxiety, and even psychosis.[55,56] Knowledge is power, and armed with knowledge, we can potentially break the chains limiting our potential by making the necessary adjustments.

Prior to implementing the steps of AOVIA, you must identify the reasons for your own pain of feeling stuck and desire a path of unlimited potential. After that, you can do the work related to asking, observing, and visualizing as discussed in the previous chapters. If you have not done so yet, you can always go back to the beginning of the book. The processing of the information, answering the questions, and completing the exercises will propel you to move forward and allow you to enjoy the resulting progress. In my case, I had to step away from my usual routine to become receptive to the formerly unknown. You must decide how much time you need and how you will support yourself until you discover a new direction.

Perhaps you have done the work but still feel lost. Please, do not give up. Sometimes the best course of action is to admit that you do not have the answer. Keeping your cup empty allows you to be in a receiving mode instead of forcing solutions. Only during my time out, new opportunities related to writing and publishing this book and working flexible hours as an independent social work contractor began to emerge. As a direct result, I developed the AOVIA Principle not only to help myself but also as a guide for anyone suffering from the pain of feeling stuck.

Often, the person who has all the answers because of *having seen the light* is the most lost. Unlimited success is tied to your highest purpose. That means that the light of your vision will forever flicker as a guide in the distance, no matter how close you get. Your movement toward that light is what counts, not the light itself. And the only way you can evaluate progress made is by knowing where you came from after reaching a milestone or specific goal on your path.

After introducing "Step #4: Implement Specific Steps Toward Your Goal" in this chapter, I will present "Step #5: Analyze Progress Made" in the next one. But first, I provide you with another "Dare to Imagine" exercise you can use to process important points from this chapter and a "Reader's Notes" page to capture your Aha! moments.

Dare to Imagine:

- The steps of asking, observing, and visualizing moving you forward.
- Visualization as looking ahead.
- Having established your goals and objectives.
- Details on how to proceed emerging while on your path.
- A new perspective of roots that transcends ancestry and includes epigenetics.
- Roots upholding the barriers of problems and flow of solutions.
- Admitting when you are stuck and becoming receptive to something new.
- Answers emerging from the previously unknown.
- Your movement toward your light counting, not the light itself.

Margrit Goodhand

Reader's Notes:

CHAPTER SEVEN
∞
ANALYZE PROGRESS MADE

I am living my dream
~Margrit Goodhand

The last step of implementing the AOVIA Principle is to analyze progress made. It is comparing where we are to where we came from. And if we "dared to imagine," our lives will show the evidence of having made progress. Coming from various backgrounds, the reasons for our specific pain may vastly differ; however, the solution I developed is of universal value. It is *The AOVIA Principle: A Path of Unlimited Potential.*

Part of our process was *asking* what type of success we want, *observing* who we are by engaging in awareness practice, *visualizing* our desired goals with preferred methods, and *implementing* specific steps toward our goal. Now we proceed to *analyzing* progress made. In the end, our very lives present the evidence how *just as children unconsciously play themselves into the future by visualizing, adults can do the same to reach desired goals.* Looking back, I am amazed, grateful, and humbled by how far I have come.

One year ago, I felt burned out, resigned from an upwardly mobile position and had no idea how to proceed. Today, I am a well-established social work contractor providing in home and telehealth therapy for seniors. One year ago, I had no book. Today, I am a published author. Additionally, I have improved the quality of my family relationships and reconnected with old friends despite the current COVID-19 pandemic by learning to use virtual means. Further, I have begun to explore my own and to assist others with their genealogy research by deciphering and translating documents written in the old German scripts of Suetterlin or Kurrent going back as far as AD 1750. Moreover, I made new friends based on shared experiences as sent-away kids and became active as the US Coordinator for Verschickungskinder living here. Finally, I was asked to translate a book that fills the gaps of a postwar German history with significant historical events.

Although the COVID-19 pandemic has prevented me from being a snowbird and leaving Florida for the summer as planned, I am living my dream because I help others to feel better by rekindling their hope and eliciting internal motivation using therapy, advocacy, and writing. My core value is compassion. In September 2021, I plan to travel to the Frisian Island of Borkum to attend a live Congress for the Verschickungskinder. It is my hope that all current travel restrictions due to COVID-19 will be lifted by then.

Today, I have a voice, a working laptop, an A-key, and plenty of paper!

Margrit Goodhand

Reader's Notes:

CHAPTER EIGHT
∞
SCRIPTS FOR SELF-HELP & TIPS FOR HAPPINESS

My final chapter provides you with scripts of "Positive Affirmations," a "Controlled Breath Meditation," a "Creative Visualization" exercise, and general "Tips for Happiness." As previously discussed, positive affirmations work best by association with a symbol that represents your stated desire. A meaningful practice is to go on a mindful treasure hunt walk and see what you can find in nature that can serve as such a symbol. Examples include feathers, pebbles, rocks, twigs, flowers, herbs, pinecones, shells, bark, etc. The following positive affirmations are responses to specific problem statements offering corresponding solutions that you may want to modify to suit your needs. While all of my scripts for self-help can be used as integrated components of hypnotherapy, each is a powerful stand-alone method to promote deep relaxation. Using them, will get you in a state of receptivity toward making your life a masterpiece.

Positive Affirmations

Examples of problems people experience are low self-esteem, lack of confidence, procrastination, or feeling stressed. Because a positive affirmation is a solution to a specific problem, you must first identify and clarify the problem in your own words. Below are examples of clear individualized problem statements with the corresponding positive affirmations following.

> Problem Statement: I put myself down a lot.
>
> Positive Affirmation: I value what I think, feel, and do.
>
> Problem Statement: I do not start new projects because I think I am going to fail.
>
> Positive Affirmation: I am successful at starting and completing new projects.
>
> Problem Statement: I push tasks off until later and then feel bad because they do not get done at all.
>
> Positive Affirmation: I complete tasks prior to deadlines and enjoy the feeling of being finished.
>
> Problem Statement: I am so stressed out that I feel like a rubber band about to snap.
>
> Positive Affirmation: I pay attention to my breathing and feel relaxed.

As previously mentioned, in order to maximize the effectiveness of a positive affirmation, you must speak it aloud while looking at a symbol that your mind can associate with the affirmation.

Controlled Breath Meditation

Take a few moments to relax and focus on your breathing. Then take a couple of deep, long breaths. Notice the cool fresh air entering your nose, filling your lungs with oxygen, warming up, and then leaving out of your mouth. Continue that breathing pattern for a while. Cool fresh air is entering your nose, filling your lungs with oxygen, and warming up as it leaves out of your mouth. Again, cool fresh air is entering your nose, filling your lungs with oxygen, and warming up as it exits your mouth.

While you keep breathing that way, you start feeling more and more relaxed. Cool fresh air is entering your nose, filling your lungs with oxygen, and warming up as it leaves out of your mouth. You are feeling even more relaxed now. As thoughts come up, do not fight them. Instead, shift your attention to your breathing. Cool fresh air is entering your nose, filling your lungs with oxygen, and warming up as it leaves your mouth. Again, cool fresh air is entering your nose, filling your lungs with oxygen, and warming up as it leaves your mouth.

Mentally scan your entire body and identify where you feel tension. Consciously relax that area now. Cool fresh air is entering your nose, filling your lungs with oxygen, and warming up as it leaves your mouth. If you feel you hear any noise coming from the environment, keep it in the background and continue to focus on your breathing. Cool fresh air is entering your nose, filling your lungs with oxygen, and warming up as it leaves out of your mouth. Breathing in … breathing out … breathing in … breathing out … breathing in … breathing out.

Again, cool fresh air is entering your nose, filling your lungs with oxygen, and warming up as it leaves your mouth. Breathing in … breathing out … breathing in … breathing out … breathing in … breathing out. You are completely relaxed now. Enjoy the feeling of deep relaxation for a couple of minutes. Then, slowly get up and go about your normal business while feeling completely rejuvenated.

Creative Beach Visualization

Imagine that you are sitting on a bench near the beach. You see a long wooden stairway, leading down toward a beautiful beach with pearly white sand and a shoreline being gently caressed by deep blue water. You wear white linen garments, are barefoot, and feel a gentle inviting breeze on your face and body.

Now you get up and walk over to the worn wooden steps. As you start walking down the stairway, you feel the wood on your soles. With each step, you feel more and more relaxed. As you continue down the stairway, your eyes follow the bright white shoreline until it disappears from your sight. The ocean is a deep blue, creating gentle crests of waves rolling toward the shore, bringing treasures from the deep waters, and then leaving again.

When you reach the bottom of the steps, your bare feet sink into the warm and soothing sand. You are melting with your environment and feel whole. The sounds of the surf get louder and calms your mind as waves crash into and over each other. You feel very, very relaxed. The sun is caressing your face and body and the wind plays with your hair. You feel invigorated by the salty smell of the air and take a couple of deep breath in and out, in … out … in … out … in … out … in … out. You feel completely at ease.

As you get to the water's edge, you invite the waves to flow over your feet, occasionally reaching your knees and then receding back into the ocean. You gaze at the distant horizon and notice two seagulls soaring above the water, their cries getting softer as they glide into the distance. The cool water feels soft and comforting as you enjoy a few moments gazing out on the far-reaching horizon. As you take in all sights, sounds, and sensations, you relax more and more.

You slowly start to walk along the shoreline near the edge of water, feeling comfortable as warm water is moving over and away from your feet. A gentle cooling breeze caresses your back. With each step, you relax more and more. You feel at one with the sights and sounds, sun, breeze, and the sand below your feet. You are really relaxed now. You see a colorful beach chair on white undisturbed sand as if waiting just for you to sit in it.

You walk over to the chair, sit down, lean back, and get comfortable. You take a deep long and slow breath in and out. Sitting in the chair, you enjoy the beautiful scenery and listen to the calming sounds. When ready, you bring your attention back to the room, and while sitting in your chair, you enjoy feeling completely calm and relaxed.

Tips for Happiness

There is nothing better than practicing a lifestyle that incorporates healthy nutrition, meaningful exercise, loving relationships, and restful sleep. In some way, we earn feeling well by engaging in these activities and, as a result, experience the effects of the feeling good chemicals serotonin, dopamine, endorphins, and oxytocin. While all of these chemicals generate positive feelings, each one has specific functions. The following sheds light on how you can make them work for you.

Serotonin is a happiness chemical. It is released during exposure to bright light, walking in nature, meditating, and thinking happy thoughts. As such, it is an effective antidepressant.

Dopamine is a rewards chemical. It is released after experiencing success such as winning at a game, completing a task, and performing acts of kindness toward others. It makes you feel like a champion.

Endorphins are pain killers. They are released after aerobic and anaerobic exercise, running and walking, and when you laugh. They are also effective in reducing depression.

Oxytocin is a love hormone. It is released by cuddling, hugging, giving compliments, and thoughts or acts of kindness. It is also effective in reducing anxiety.

Neglecting our well-being or abusing our bodies leads to deficiencies. These includes substance abuse during which the production of the feeling good chemicals is interrupted because the body gets them from the outside; that can lead to developing tolerance and addiction. That is why addicts feel poorly for an extended period of time—even after detoxification—until they make the necessary lifestyle adjustments and give their bodies and minds a chance to recover.

EPILOGUE

I am finished writing and you are finished reading *The AOVIA Principle: A Path of Unlimited Potential*. As a result of processing the information and completing the assignments and exercises, we have learned how to enlist the areas beneath our ordinary consciousness to move forward on a path of unlimited potential. We have established our visions, identified our core values, clarified what type of success we want, and established our goals and objectives for the way. Our visions guide us towards a beckoning light and our core values drive us on a path of unlimited potential.

Further, we have learned to become receptive to the emergence of synchronistic events aiding us and developed skills to transcend barriers on our way. We have experienced a taste of unlimited success, and, as a direct result of that success, developed an attitude that makes us unstoppable. We feel empowered by experiencing our individual lives evolving as masterpieces as they were destined to be!

Since I fully embraced that six-year old child within me, validated her suffering, and honored her attempts to play herself into the future by visualizing herself as a therapist and writer, too many good things have happened to fit into an epilogue. It suffices to say that *I am finally living my dream* and plan to write a novel next. Growing up in the West, I also have roots in the East; this presents a fertile ground for my imagination. Further, I plan travel to the Frisian Island of Borkum in order to attend the next live Verschickungskinder Congress in September 2021 unless prevented by travel restrictions because of the COVID-19 epidemic.

This time, when walking on the beaches of the North Sea, I will be prepared to easily move through the high sands against a fresh wind on my face and a new perspective. My vision is clear, my voice is strong, and my mind is open ….

ABOUT THE AUTHOR

Margrit Goodhand is an LCSW and CAP practicing in Florida as an independent social work contractor. She began freelance writing during the 1980s while living in Pennsylvania, publishing non-fiction pieces in *The Daily News, Women's Household, Women's World*, and *Community Magazine*. In 1988, Margrit won first prize at the Harrisburg Manuscript Club in the Jean Allen Grey Memorial Award Category. She writes non-fiction and fiction. One of her short stories was published in *The Best of Dunedin Writers Group 2019: An Anthology*. *The AOVIA Principle: A Path of Unlimited Potential* is her first book. Margrit can be reached at therapynbooks@gmail.com.

ENDNOTES

1. Miller, 1990 (9, 59).
2. Roehl, n.d. Trauma.
3. Wendt, 2015 (291-292).
4. Angelou, n.d. Brainy Quote.
5. McLeod, 2015.
6. McLeod, 2018.
7. Brenner, 2018.
8. Miller, 1990.
9. Roehl, n.d. "Shipments of Children."
10. Knight, 2020.
11. Roehl, n.d. "Borkum Kongress."
12. Chopra, 2003 (28-32).
13. McLeod, 2018.
14. Tolle, 2016 (31-33).
15. Jelinek, 2015.
16. Joseph, Unconditional Positive Regard. (29)

17 Lama, n.d. Biography.

18 Lama, n.d. BrainyQuote.

19 Utah Historical Review, 2011.

20 Haven, 2010.

21 Brown, 2020.

22 Lama, n.d. Schedule.

23 Coleman and Davidson, 2018.

24 Mindvalley, 2018.

25 Waxman, 2018.

26 Angelou, 2018.

27 Collins, 2005, (21-22).

28 Collins, 2004, (xi-xvi).

29 Maier and Seligman, 2016.

30 Joshi and Mangette, 2018.

31 Wallin, 2020.

32 Belludi, 2008.

33 Cohen, n.d.

34 Tzu, n.d.

35 Wendt, 2015 (15).

36 Ibid, (190-191).

37 Lazarus, 2019.

38 Chopra, 2003 (22-32).

39 Jung, 1972.

40 Fierke, 2017 (141-169).

41 Upadhyay et al., 2016.

42 Coleman and Davidson, 2018.

43 Staff Editorial, 2013.

44 Bygraves, 2019.

45 Alston, 2020.

46 Huang and Charyton, 2008 (38).

47 Nielsson, 2010.

48 Ganis et al., 2003.

49 De Bono, 2016.

50 Mongiovi, 2014.

51 Stewart, 2005.

52 Wobst, 2007.

53 Byrne, 2019.

54 Forbes, 2001.

55 Powledge, 2011 (588-592).

56 Pishva et al., 2014.

BIBLIOGRAPHY

Alston, T. (2020, June 05). Three Elite Performers Using Neurofeedback: Tracy Alston. Retrieved October 01, 2020, from https://tracyalston.com/elite-performers-using-neurofeedback/

Angelou, Maya. (n.d.) *BrainyQuote.com, BrainyMedia Inc. 2020.*

Angelou, Maya. (2018). *Supersoul Sunday with Oprah Winfrey.* https://www.facebook.com/SuperSoulSunday/videos/1812625085451670.

Belludi, Nagesh. (2008, October 10). *Right Attitudes.* https://www.rightattitudes.com/2008/10/04/7-38-55-rule-personal-communication/.

Brenner, Grant Hilary MD, FAPA. (2018, September 09). "Is Projection the Most Powerful Defense Mechanism?" *Psychology Today.* https://www.psychologytoday.com/us/experts/grant-hilary-brenner-md-fapa.

Brown, Kara Jillian. (2020, July 06). "6 Tips for Longevity From the Dalai Lama on his 85th Birthday." *MSN Lifestyle.* https://www.msn.com/en-us/health/wellness/6-tips-for-longevity.

Bygraves, Maisie. (2019, July 19). "Peak." *You Should Treat Your Brain LIke a Muscle.* https://blog.peal.net/2019/07/19/is-your-brain-a-muscle/.

Byrne, Jason. (2019). "False Cliché: Every Journey Begins with a Single Step." *FloSports Engineering.* https://engineering.flosports.tv/false-cliche-every-journey-begins-with-a-first-step-f0bac2f04e41.

Chopra, Deepak. (2003). *The Essential Spontaneous Fulfillment of Desire.* New York, New York: Harmony Books.

Cohen, Leonard. (n.d.) *Goodreads.* Accessed July 23, 2020. https://www.goodreads.com/quotes/4484-there-is-a-crack-in-everything-thats-how-the-light.

Coleman, Daniel and Davidson, Richard. (2018, May 07). *How Meditation Changes Your Brain-and Your Life.* https://www.lionsroar.com/how-meditation-changes-your-brain-and-your-life/.

Collins, James C. (2005). *Good to Great: Why Some Companies Make the Leap and Other Don't.* New York: New York: HarperCollins Publishers. 17-22.

Collins, Jim. (2004). "The Highest Goal." In *The Highest Goal*, by Michael Ray, xii-xvi. San Francisco, CA: Berrett-Koehler Publishers. Inc.

De Bono, Edward. (2016). "Lateral Thinking is the Step by Step approach to Creativity." *Edward De Bono.* Accessed September 12, 2020. https://www.edwddebono.com/lateral-thinking.

Fierke, K. M. (2017). "Consciousness at the Interface: Wendt, Eastern Wisdom and the Ethics of Intra-action." *Critical*

Review 29, no. 2. : 141-169. doi/10.1080/08913811.2017.1319100.

Forbes, Jack. (2001). *Indigenous Americans: Spirituality and Ethos.* https://www.amacad.org/publication/indigenous-americans-spirituality-and-ethos.

Ganis, Giorgio, William L. Thompson, Fred W. Mast, and Stephen M. Kosslyn. (2003, August 01). "Visual imagery in cerebral visual dysfunction." *Neurologic Clinics* 21, no. 3 : 631-646. http://nmr.mgh.harvard.edu/~ganis/pdfs/gg-vision and the brain.pdf.

Haven, Cynthia. (2010, 2013, October). "Stanford's Center for Compassion and Altruism Research and Education (CCARE)." *Why the Dalai Lama Comes to Stanford.* http://ccare.stanford.edu.

Huang, Tina L., and Christine Charyton. (2008). "A Comprehensive Review of the Psychological Effects of Brainwave Entrainment." *Alternative Therapies in Health and Medicine* 14 no. 5:38. https://ncbi.nlm.nih.gov/pubmed/18780583.

Jelinek, Elizabeth Maureen. (2015). *Epigenetics: The Transgenerational Transmission of Ancestral Trauma, Experiences, and Behaviors—As Seen in Systemic Family Constellations.*" Phd Thesis, ResearchGate. http://gradworks.umi.com/37/26/3726301.html.

Joseph, Stephen Ph.D. (2012, October 07). "Unconditional Positive Regard." *Psychology Today.* https://www.

psychologytoday.com/us/blog/what-doesnt-kill-us/201210/unconditional-positive-regard.

Joshi, Aishwarya, and Haley, Mangette. (2018, April 03). "Unmasking of Impostor Syndrome." *ResearchGate.* https://ecommons.udayton.edu/jraphe/vol3/iss1/3.

Jung, Carl. (1972). *Synchronicity – An Acausal Connecting Principle.* Routledge and Kegan Paul.

Knight, Ben. (2020, October 10). "Nazi War Criminals ran children's homes in postwar Germany, new research." *Verschickungen.* https://www.verschickungsheime.de.

Lama, Dalai. (n.d.) „Dalai Lama Quotes." *BrainyQuote.com, BrainyMedia Inc, 2020.* Accessed July 21, 2020. https://www.brainyquote.com/quotes/dalai_lama_101711.

Lazarus, Clifford N. (2019, June 26). "Does Consciousness Exist Outside the Brain." *Psychology Today.* https://www.psychologytoday.com/us/blog/think-well/201906/does-consciousness-exist-outside-the-brain?amp.

Maier, Stephen F., Seligman, Martin E. P. (2016, July). "Psychological Review." 349-367. doi:10.1037/rev0000033.

McLeod, S. A. (2018, May 21). "Carl Jung." *SimplyPsychology.* https://www.simplypsychology.org/carl-jung.html.

McLeod, S.A. (2015). "Freud and the Unconscious Mind." *Simply Psychology.* www.simplypsychology.org/unconscious-mind.html.

Miller, Alice. (1990). "Poisonous Pedagogy." In *For Your Own Good*, by Alice Miller. New York, New York: The Noonday Press. 3-102.

Mindvalley. (2018, August 07). "Brainwave States: Accessing Your Brain's True Capacity." *Mindvalley*. https://blog.mindvalley.com/brain-waves.

Mongiovi, John. (2014, October 22). "A History of Hypnosis: From Ancient Times to Modern Psychology." http://www.johnmongovi.com/blog/2014/10/22/a-history-of-hypnosis-from-ancient-temples-to-modern-psychology.

Nielsson, Jeff. (2010, March 06). "Albert Einstein: Imagination is more important than knowledge." *The Saturday Evening Post*. https://www.saturdayeveningpost.com/2010/03/imagination-important-knowledge/.

Pishva, Ehsan, Marjan Drukker, Wolfgang Viechtbauer, Jeroen Decoster, Dina Collip, Ruud van Winkel, Marieke Wichers, et al. (2014). "Epigenetic Genes and Emotional Reactivity to Daily Life Events: A Multi-Step Gene-Environment Interaction Study." *PLOS ONE* 9 no. 6. https://journals.plos.org/plosone/article?id=10.1371/journal.pone.0100935.

Powledge, Tabitha M. (2011). "Behavioral Epigenetics: How Nurture Shapes Nature." *BioScience*, 61 no. 8: 588-592. https://academic.oup.com/bioscience/article/61/8/588/336969.

Roehl, Anja. (n.d.) „Das Trauma der Verschickungskinder." *Verschickungsheime*. Accessed July 23, 2020. https://www.verschickungsheime.de.

—"Kongress 2020 auf Borkum." (n.d.) *Verschickungsheime.* Accessed September 23, 2020. https://www.verschickungsheime.de.

—"Verschickungen or Shipments of Children (from 1950-1990) a Trauma to This Day." (n.d.) *Verschickungsheime.* Accessed July 23, 2020. https://www.verschickungsheime.de.

Staff, Editorial. (2013). "Train Your Brain Like a Muscle." *To Your Health.* October, 2013. https://www.toyourhealth.com/mpacms/tyh/article.php?id=1885.

Stewart, James H. (2005, April 01). "Hypnosis in Contemporary Medicine." *Mayo Clinic Proceedings.* 80 n. 4 . doi:https://doi.org/10.4065/80.4.511.

The Office of His Holiness the Dalai Lama. (n.d.) "Brief Biography." *His Holiness The 14th Dalai Lama of Tibet.* Accessed July 21, 2020. https://www.dalailama.com/the-dalai-lama/biography-and-daily-life/brief-schedule.

The Office of his Holiness the Dalai Lama. (n.d.) "Schedule." *His Holiness the 14th Dalai Lama of Tibet.* Accessed July 21, 2020, https://www.dalailama.com/schedule.

Tolle, Eckhart. (2016). *A New Earth: Awakening to Your Life's Purpose.* New York, New York: Penguin Books. 30-33.

Tzu, Lao. (n.d.) "Spiritual Wisdom Quotes." *Goodreads.* Accessed July 26, 2020. https://www.goodreads.com/quotes/964169-lao-tzu-the-key-to-growth-is-the-introduction-of.

Upadhyay, M R, Chen W, Lenstra J A, Goderie C R J, MacHugh D E, Park SDE, Magee D A, Matassino D, Ciani F, Megens H-J. (2016). "Genetic Origin, admixture and population history of aurochs (bos primigenious) and primitive Euopean cattle." *Heredity* 118, 169-176. Accessed July 23, 2020. https://doi.org/10.1038/hdy.2016.79.

Utah Historical Review. (2011). The Alpha Rho Papers. "The Argument over Reincarnation in Early Christianity." Historia: The Alpha Row Papers. 1. https://epubs.utah.edu/index/php/historia/article/view/578.

Wallin, Emmi. (2020). "Dalai Lama Net Worth." *Wealthy Gorilla.* Accessed July 23, 2020. https://wealthygorilla.com/dalai-lama-net-worth/.

Waxman, Olivia. (2018, April 04). "5 Things to Know About Maya Angelou's Complicated Meaningful Life." *Time Magazine.* Accessed July 26, 2020. https://www.history.com/this-day-in-history/maya-angelou-is-born.

Wendt, Alexander. (2015). *Quantum Mind and Social Science.* Cambridge: Cambridge University Press.

Wobst, Albrecht. (2007, May). *Anesthesia & Analgesics, 104, No. 5. : 1199-1208.* https://journals.lww.com/anesthesia-analgesia/pages/articleviewer.aspx?year=2007&issue=05000&article=00036&type=Fulltext.

www.ingramcontent.com/pod-product-compliance
Lightning Source LLC
LaVergne TN
LVHW091549060526
838200LV00036B/763